The English Language and Images of Matter

LANGUAGE AND LANGUAGE LEARNING

General Editors: RONALD MACKIN *and* PETER STREVENS

The English Language and Images of Matter

RANDOLPH QUIRK

RXTSA

OXFORD UNIVERSITY PRESS

LONDON 1972

Oxford University Press, Ely House, London W.1

GLASGOW NEW YORK TORONTO MELBOURNE WELLINGTON
CAPE TOWN IBADAN NAIROBI DAR ES SALAAM LUSAKA ADDIS ABABA
DELHI BOMBAY CALCUTTA MADRAS KARACHI LAHORE DACCA
KUALA LUMPUR SINGAPORE HONG KONG TOKYO

Library Edition ISBN 0 19 437121 2
Paperback Edition ISBN 0 19 437056 9

SET BY THE LANCASHIRE TYPESETTING CO. LTD. AND PRINTED IN GREAT BRITAIN
BY LATIMER TREND & CO. LTD., WHITSTABLE

Contents

Preface

Although nearly half of the material in this book has appeared elsewhere, there seems to be good justification for reprinting these papers along with the new ones. In the first place, they are not for the most part easily accessible. Secondly, one welcomes an opportunity to introduce much desirable correction and revision. But most of all, their complementary relationship is otherwise well-nigh impossible to demonstrate.

There is more to language than social concerns, but man's involvement with personal and local identity, with the issues of national politics, with the whole complex web of society, bites deep into language and at the same time conditions in large measure the extent to which one is personally conscious of language at all. It is true that this consciousness can frequently be seen as a retreat from content to expression, from 'matter' to 'words', an unabating perversion by which man's linguistic energies are deflected from intellectual creativity to cosmetic delusion:

> *Mephistopheles:* . . . to words stick fast!
> Then through a sure gate you'll at last
> Enter the templed hall of Certainty.
>
> *Student:* Yet in each word some concept there must be.
>
> *Mephistopheles:* Quite true! But don't torment yourself too anxiously;
> For at the point where concepts fail,
> At the right time a word is thrust in there.
> With words we fitly can our foes assail,
> With words a system we prepare,
> Words we quite fitly can believe.
> Nor from a word a mere iota thieve.
>
> (Goethe, *Faust* I. 1900ff, tr. G. M. Priest)

. . . men began to hunt more after words than . . . weight of matter, worth of subject, soundness of argument, life of invention, or depth of judgement . . . It seems to me that Pygmalion's frenzy is a good emblem or portraiture of this vanity: for words are but the images of matter; and except they have life of reason and invention, to fall in love with them is all one as to fall in love with a picture.

(Bacon, *Advancement of Learning* I.iv,2–3)

But the concerns of ordinary people with language can be seen in a less negative and a more charitable light. A lively interest in the word can reflect not a vanity but an insistent and urgent need to grapple with and encapsulate man's stubbornest, most deep-seated longings, from an elusive dream to a bitter reality.

In this book, attention is given in several chapters to questions of language variation as it affects political and social alignments, the advancement of underdeveloped peoples, and the teaching of English as a world language. The relations between British and American English are explored in some detail, not merely in respect of what differentiates and what unites these two great varieties of English, but from the viewpoint of the cultural, political and educational factors that have determined their intimately interwoven history over the past two or three hundred years. At the opposite extreme, there is a study of what happens when English is stripped down to wrestle nakedly with the needs of men communicating only on the most elemental level of practical commerce: and of what potential such a pidgin variety of language has when it is obliged to carry wider responsibilities.

Between these extremes there are the concerns of the ordinary native speaker of English, interested chiefly in the language of his own society—its quality, its structure, and the impact upon it of social and environmental change. Several of the chapters are devoted to aspects of contemporary English, arising from work on the Survey of English Usage over the past ten or twelve years. The Survey, an on-going activity in the English Department of University College London, has as its field of inquiry the wide-ranging repertoire, in speech and writing, of the educated native English speaker today. Our objectives include a continuously enhanced file of taped, manuscript and printed materials, accessible in grammatically analysed form, representing a wide range of inter-personal relationships and of subject matter; a psycho- and sociolinguistic inquiry into the native speaker's linguistic potential and into his reaction to variant English forms; the production of published studies distilling our experience and probing special difficulties. While the problems and methods of grammatical description are inevitably different from those of lexicological description, the standards of scholarship and the goals in coverage can be similar. We seek to provide an authoritative account of English grammatical usage to match (in all respects except the historical dimension) the Oxford English Dictionary's continually updated study of lexical usage. The SEU, which has enjoyed financial help from a number of sources since its inception in 1960, is at present supported by grants from the Leverhulme Trust and the Calouste Gulbenkian Foundation for which my colleagues and I are deeply grateful.

In preparing the present volume, I greatly benefited from General Editorial help at its most sensitive and perceptive. As a result individual chapters have been improved, as well as the relations between them.

RQ

University College London
January 1972

1 Philology, Politics, and American English

Even before Sir William Jones convinced his Bombay audience in 1786 of the common origin of Sanskrit, Greek and Latin, scholars had been well aware that one language could give rise to many different languages in the course of physical and temporal separation. How else to explain Babel and the confusion of tongues? But with the nineteenth century, plotting the fissiparousness of languages became virtually a philological obsession. With good reason. One now saw rather precisely how a common Slavic resembling Old Church Slavonic had become Russian, Polish, Bulgarian, Czech, Slovak, Serbian and the rest; how a Germanic resembling Gothic had given way to still more sharply differentiated languages such as English, Icelandic and German; how with the death of the Roman Empire, Latin had withdrawn into semi-retirement, leaving sons like Rumanian, French and Spanish that did not speak to each other.

With such paradigms from the past, philologists naturally speculated on the probable fate of contemporary languages. And surely it was right to see it as the probable fate. European imperialism had taken western Indo-European vernaculars all round the globe. To name a few examples, there was Dutch in South America and South East Asia; French in Canada, Africa and the West Indies; Spanish in Central and South America; Portuguese in Africa and Brazil; and English everywhere. Why should these tongues not proliferate as their own parents, Germanic and Latin, had proliferated? The nineteenth century had good reason to expect profusion and independent development, idealizing nationalism with almost as maniacal a fervour as we have done in our own generation, and lacking our easy and rapid means of communication which can send men round the globe almost as speedily as radio messages or ballistic missiles. Was it not inevitable, as night follows day (the death and corruption emphasis) or as day follows night (the regeneration emphasis), that a new language Brazilian would be incomprehensible in Oporto, a Québecois remote from the sober guidance of the Académie? And South of the St Lawrence, as we read in Fennimore Cooper (1828), 'an entirely different standard for the language must be established . . . from that which governs so absolutely in England' so that according to Webster (1800), differences would 'multiply and render it necessary that we should have Dictionaries of the *American language*'.[1]

Some informed opinion in Britain was in full agreement. Writing not long before his death in 1804, it seemed to Jonathan Boucher that Americans were 'peculiarly addicted to innovation', and were 'making all the haste they conveniently can, to rid themselves' of a common language with the old country. In consequence, 'it is easy to foresee that, in no very distant period, their language will become as independent of England, as they themselves are; and altogether as unlike English, as the Dutch or Flemish is unlike German . . .'

It is of course too soon to pronounce on the extent to which these eighteenth- and nineteenth-century predictions are to be vindicated by history. Hardly 400 years have elapsed since the Age of Exploration began to disperse European tongues around the world, and this is a very short period in terms of linguistic change. Moreover, so far as French and English in North America are concerned, it is much less than 400 years—little more than 300—since colonization took place in sufficient numbers to give a reasonable chance of forming a stable linguistic community. We may however ask whether, within these severe limitations, divisive linguistic developments have taken place in the English language, such as to confirm the separatist predictions.

The answer is certainly 'Yes'. We shall return and qualify this answer presently but there is good evidence as early as the eighteenth century that Britons and Americans recognized each other's speech as characteristically different. Such differences multipled rather rapidly during the nineteenth century so that along with a few grammatical and phonological distinctions there were large numbers of lexical items sharply indicating separate development. This was, naturally enough, especially true of terms for the new technology that was developing more or less independently on both sides of the Atlantic. Two groups of transport terms will illustrate this.

AmE:	BrE:
box car	goods van
caboose	brake (or guard's) van
car	coach (but dining *car*)
conductor	guard
hood	bonnet

muffler	silencer
oil pan	sump
sedan	saloon

Very considerable lexical differences had sprung up long before sets like these evolved, but in grammar members of the two communities had less to remark on. The industrious John Pickering of Boston, *Vocabulary or Collection of Words and Phrases* (1816), could detect little more impressive than a difference in the locative use of prepositions (*to Philadelphia* where British usage would prefer *in* or *at*). And Dickens in all the savagery of his attack on American English (especially in *Chuzzlewit*, 1843) virtually ignored features of grammar. Not even the most widely known of current Anglo-American differences in this area, *gotten*, appears to have thrust itself on his consciousness in the linguistic onsets he appears to have suffered during his visit of 1842. What does the Dickensian caricature in fact suggest, then? That the most noticeable (or reprehensible) aspects of American English lay in pronunciation, prosody, and lexical style: occasionally lexical items that are wholly unfamiliar; but for the most part it is merely a matter of stylistic oddness—especially, a monotonous pomposity:

> You are now, Sir, a denizen of the most powerful and highly-civilized do-minion that has ever graced the world; a do-minion, Sir, where man is bound to man in one vast bond of equal love and truth. May you, Sir, be worthy of your a-dopted country! (*Chuzzlewit* Ch. 21)

Divisiveness, in short, was certainly in evidence but it was a divisiveness that showed itself in rather trifling respects and one that even so was subject to gross exaggeration and distortion by commentators who rarely managed—rarely enough attempted— to record objective observations unmediated by political or social prejudice. There is a lamentable human tendency to laugh and sneer at the other man's language that we cannot understand. But things are worse still when we completely understand what he is saying and can concentrate our envenomed ridicule on how he is saying it. This is one of the commonest superficial grounds for friction within a country, within a township, within a street: even within a single home. Between larger communities, it is a common reason for 'institutionalizing' a new language: why tolerate being told you speak someone else's language badly when by a simple declarative act you can be acknowledged as speaking your own perfectly?

A 'Philological Society of New York' was set up in 1788 with 'the purpose of ascertaining and improving the *American Tongue*' and it proceeded to rough out 'the principles of a *Federal* language' for the ten young United States. If its hopes were short lived they were hopes that were frequently regenerate, and though American desire for linguistic self-respect is not of course the reason for differences between American and British English, it has nevertheless considerably influenced much of the fiction about American English—and perhaps some of the fact. Let us take, for instance, the claim that American English is characteristically *uniform* as compared with British English. To the extent that this is true, it is largely a matter of what we would expect from a number of important and well established factors.

First, the comparative uniformity of the earlier settlers' speech having a larger than average proportion of educated use and reflecting the tendency already present in seventeenth century Britain for educated people to have a concept of standard English, transcending regional dialects. As Webster remarked in 1836, 'Many of the principal emigrants to this country, on its first settlement, were educated at the English Universities, and they brought with them the purest pronunciation of the language'. At any rate the early settlers did not simply represent a cross section of the broad dialect speakers of the areas from which they came. Secondly, the 350 years of America's settlement have not been favourable to a marked growth of dialect because this period has witnessed a steadily growing and radically changing development in communication—in mobility of population particularly. Moreover, a well-known charactersitic of American life is the readiness of whole families to migrate over vast distances and of course to take all cultural habits including speech wherever they go. This has caused a remarkable cultural evenness—in eating, building, social habits and speech—over the whole country. Life is not isolated, village by village, as it tends to be in Europe. This even distribution of habits has of course been reinforced in recent years by radio, television, and the still greater ease of movement by road, rail and air. Thirdly, we have the tendency to uniformity reinforced by the education system. Being so long established in the United States, education has been able to influence speech habits quite markedly, and it has been strongly supported by social and political factors. The democratic republican system from its inception was a denial of the prestige of court and squire: 'Jack's as good as the next man', or rather he *can* be—not through birth or by imitation of the socially fashionable but by a rational use of *knowledge, a conscious skill* that can be anyone's for the asking. The grammarian and the lexicographer and their executive official, the schoolteacher, were the only proper arbiters of linguistic correctness. This attitude is common enough in all civilized countries, of course. Writing less than a generation from the beginning of universal elementary education in England, Thomas Hardy was able to contrast Tess and her mother in this respect:

> Mrs Durbeyfield habitually spoke the dialect; her daughter, who had passed the Sixth Standard in the National School under a London-trained mistress, spoke two languages; the dialect at home, more or less; ordinary English abroad and to persons of quality.

But nowhere has the attitude been more deeply engrained than in America. Even though the mass of Americans don't in fact speak according to the book they have a well drilled knowledge of what the book says and a clear notion of what they ought to be speaking, and this ideal form of speech (which naturally many think they *are* using) is uniform.

Then again, American dialects have had only three or four hundred years to develop: British dialects have had nearly four times as long—and this is to reckon on their development only within England. That is, we have good reason to believe that English in England started with dialectal demarcation corresponding to the different areas of the Germanic continent from which groups of settlers came, preserving their identity to a significant extent. There is very little analogy to this in either the grouped provenance or grouped settlement of English speakers in the New World. At the risk of gross oversimplification it can be said that English was established in America, whether in New England or Virginia, by settlers whose English—to the extent that it was dialectal—was predominantly influenced by south-eastern British speech. It was this English which constituted the basis for imitation by the waves of subsequent settlers. The only long-term group modification of this basis seems to have occurred in the eighteenth century with the concentration of Scots, Irish and northern English settlers in what are now the states of New York and Ohio. It was the English so modified that was later carried westwards, funnelling out to become the dominant ('Midland') form of modern American English. But all the evidence suggests that the basis was already so firm as to preclude any very radical modification and the distinction drawn between the dialectal base line in Anglo-Saxon England and that in the 'American colonies' remains clear.

This implies—correctly—that, though the differences may be small by European standards, the English of America is of course by no means uniform. Regional dialects are especially well-established in the states along the Atlantic seaboard where there has been longest English-speaking settlement. Midland speakers

in Pennsylvania and New York pronounce the *r* or have an
'*r*-coloured' vowel in such words as *bird* but are flanked by
Eastern speakers in the New England states and by Southern
speakers in such states as Virginia who often have no *r*-sound in
these words. Midland speakers have an unrounded vowel in *rock*,
hot and similar words, where Easterners have a tendency towards
the kind of rounding we find in most British versions of such
words. The diphthongs of *I'm nine* would sound rather similar in
Midland, Eastern and typical British pronunciation, where
Southern speakers would tend to prolong the first part of each
diphthong so as almost to sound like 'ahm nahn'. In addition to
the North American dialects here mentioned, one should of course
add Canadian English which, though closely resembling the
corresponding American English dialects along the 3000-mile
frontier, has certain important characteristics of its own.

The dialectal differences do not reside solely in pronunciation
but affect grammar and vocabulary as well. While many people
along the Atlantic seaboard have *dived* as the past of *dive*, almost
as many say *dove*. What most people call a *pancake*, some
Midland and Southern speakers call a *flannelcake*; what is called
a *soft drink* in most places is called a *tonic* by some Eastern
speakers.

It will be noticed that with nearly all these regional differences,
British speech tends to agree with one or other of the American
dialects. It is in fact rather rare to find all American speakers in
agreement with each other while being in disagreement with all
British speakers. The isoglosses more frequently run east and west
across the Atlantic rather than—as it were—down the middle, a
given feature being held in common between an American and a
British dialect and absent from other dialects in the two major
areas. This is true even of 'post-vocalic *r*': it does not distinguish
American from British speech so much as Midland American
from the speech of eastern and south-eastern England. Here is an
aspect of Anglo-American linguistic relations to which we shall
return.

Nothing said above must seem to equate the dialectal differences in North America with the much more radical ones in the
British Isles where major divisions like Scots, Anglo-Irish, North
country, Midland, London misleadingly obscure the fact that
there are deeper divisions between for example the various North
country dialects of England than there are between all the American ones. Nor must language diversity in Britain or America be
seen solely in terms of regional dialect. Educational and social
status—not to mention racial grouping—produce widespread
variation between say Queens, Brooklyn, Harlem and Lower East-

side in New York and between say Hampstead, Hounslow and Stepney in London. And in this matter of social as opposed to regional variation, it would be very rash indeed to suppose that there is more uniformity in American than in British English. Here again, incidentally, Anglo-American links often strikingly dismiss the Atlantic as a linguistic frontier: American and British teenagers have a wide range of language in common which parents (and more especially grandparents) on each side of the Atlantic fail alike to share.

Yet the image of a uniform American English sharply contrasting as a whole with any part of the extremely heterogeneous English of Britain is one that has seemed soundly based for more than two centuries by observers in both communities. On the British side, of course, there must always be a danger that this is due in part to the relative rarity of the phenomenon observed: most of us see more variation among horses than among camels. The illusion could also be readily fed by political or philosophical predisposition. If you thought uniformity was the rational development for a nation and if with Whig sympathies you approved of American independence, you saw good and uniform English providing unity across groups in widely separated states and from different social and racial backgrounds. Less frequently (and usually more recently) it has worked the other way. If you disapproved of cultural levelling and saw American social development as a vulgarization process, you could ignore evidence of linguistic variety and fasten on that of linguistic uniformity as a deplorable emblem of an orthodoxy-haunted herd spirit.

Approving if surprised and sometimes patronizing comments by British observers are not uncommon even before the War of Independence. On a five-year experience of Virginia, Hugh Jones wrote in 1724 that 'the *Planters*, and even the *Native Negroes* generally talk good *English* without *Idiom* or *Tone*'—that is, without dialectal peculiarities. In a letter written by William Eddis in June 1770, the British and American situation are explicitly compared:

> In England, almost every county is distinguished by a peculiar dialect;
> ... but in Maryland, and throughout adjacent provinces, it is worthy
> of observation, that a striking similarity of speech universally prevails
> ... The language ... is perfectly uniform, and unadulterated; nor has
> it borrowed any provincial, or national accent, from its British or
> foreign parentage.

Several observers pointed out that the language was not only uniform but uniformly good, and that this transcended class barriers as well as geographical ones. Lord Adam Gordon kept a journal of his travels in 1764–5 and wrote of Philadelphia that 'the propriety of Language here surprized me much, the English tongue being spoken by all ranks, in a degree of purity and perfection, surpassing any, but the polite part of London'. In an almost contemporary diary (July 1777), Nicholas Cresswell noted:

> Though the inhabitants of this Country are composed of different Nations and different languages, yet it is very remarkable that they in general speak better English than the English do. No County or Colonial dialect is to be distinguished here . . .

though he adds that New Englanders appear to have a characteristic 'whining cadence'. In the same year, Jonathan Boucher, who lived in Maryland for sixteen years before the Revolution, noted in a letter that 'there prevails not only, I believe, the purest Pronunciation of the English Tongue that is anywhere to be met with, but a perfect Uniformity'. Similarly, to John Harriott, who went to America in 1793, it seemed that English was 'better spoken by the whole mass of people, from Georgia to Quebec, (an extent of country more than 1200 miles) than by the bulk of people in the different counties of England'.

A half-century later, and we have the same story from T. H. James's *Rambles* of 1845 when, without 'partiality to the Republicans', he reported that 'our language is spoken much better and more correctly in all parts of America than it is in England. There are no provincialisms in the States, where the abominable dialects of Somerset, York, and Lancaster, entirely disappear; and, extensive as the country is, one uniform correctness obtains . . .' In the twentieth century, too, observers have noted the relative stability and uniformity of American English, despite the enormous distances together with a large and heterogeneous population, as compared with British English, relatively deep riven with regional and class differences. In 1927, J. H. G. Grattan (*Review of English Studies*, vol. 3) attributes this situation to the fact that 'America has had an experience of universal education longer by at least two centuries than our own experience; she has met and conquered, in her vast alien population, far greater tides of linguistic barbarism than any we know here; she has been forced by circumstances to give more attention to the conscious cultivation of language than has hitherto been necessary in Great Britain . . .' In short, 'the risk of linguistic "disintegration" appears to be greater in England than in the United States'.

The image created in Britain of a uniform and unified American English was not, as we have seen, unrelated to political sympathies. Not surprisingly, the image building in America was still more strongly and overtly motivated by political considerations.

Views no less extreme and uncompromising than those of Grattan just quoted, both on the linguistic situation and on its causes, became virtually orthodox among American commentators. Addressing a British audience through the pages of the *Athenaeum* in 1835, Timothy Flint of Cincinnati wrote as follows (italics mine):

> We have not a doubt, that the first remark which would be suggested to an honest, intelligent, and philosophical British observer, in travelling from Passamaquoddy to the Sabine, would be the uniformity of phrase upon similar subjects, in which *all classes of people* would be heard to express themselves . . .
>
> Whence is this wonderful uniformity, *this unquestionable general correctness* in the use of the English language among a people . . . spread over such an immense surface, in pursuits, condition, and training, so various, as those of the lumberers of Maine, the wheat growers of the middle states, the tobacco planters of Virginia and Kentucky, and the cultivators of cotton and cane in the South, with copious sprinklings of *Dutch, German, and French emigrants* permanently fixed among them? The Anglo-Americans are a busy, bustling, moving, enterprising, *ever-travelling people*, with a temperament inclining them to a sort of ubiquity. Their perpetually recurring *elections*, the necessity under which every young man, in whose breast is the slightest germ of ambition, finds himself placed, to be always ready to put forth an harangue adapted to the emergency, . . . *the universal diffusion of common schools* . . . —in a word, the whole motive, impulse, and business of the people place him in a severe school, where words are the grand material . . .

Here we have all the elements of the reality and the ideal and the conditions making realization of the ideal so important: enormous areas, heterogeneous masses, and the hope of achieving a unified classless society through universal education, mobility of population, the democratic process of government—and a common language. As Noah Webster wrote in a letter in 1786, 'A national language is a national tie, and what country wants it more than America?'

Whatever natural conditions were tending towards a homogeneous English, it was an urgent goal to be pursued for political and philosophic reasons. Standards of language could not (so it is argued in Fennimore Cooper's *Notions of the Americans*, 1828) emanate from 'a fashionable aristocracy', from a royal court, as they were allowed to do in England: 'we are reduced to the necessity of consulting reason . . . and all the known laws of language, in order to arrive at our object'. The *Edinburgh Review* had long before (October 1809) castigated the kind of homogeneity that might allegedly proceed from such a policy: 'an utter disregard of all distinction between what we should call lofty and elegant, and low and vulgar expressions. These republican literati seem to make it a point of conscience to have no aristocratical distinctions —even in their vocabulary.'

When the reviewer was writing, there had been moves afoot in America for more than a generation to ensure that 'aristocratical distinctions' could be replaced by more rational principles to determine taste in language. Not the first such move—but equally not the least distinguished—was made in 1780 by the man who some years later was to become the Second President of the United States, John Adams. His plan, directly echoing Swift's *Proposal* of 1712, was that the authority of Congress should underwrite the national character of America's language:

> The honor of forming the first public institution for refining, correcting, improving, and ascertaining the English language, I hope is reserved for congress; they have every motive that can possibly influence a public assembly to undertake it. It will have a happy effect upon the union of the States to have a public standard for all persons in every part of the continent to appeal to, both for the signification and pronunciation of the language . . . I would therefore submit to the consideration of congress the expediency and policy of erecting by their authority a society under the name of 'the American Academy for refining, improving, and ascertaining the English Language.' The authority of congress is necessary to give such a society reputation, influence, and authority through all the states and with other nations.

Over the next 150 years there were numerous proposals, several of them considerably more radical. In 1788 there was formed the Philological Society of New York with the aim of 'ascertaining and improving the *American Tongue*,' bringing republican *apartheid* to bear upon Swiftian rationalism. In 1815 John Pickering tried to canalize the energies of the American Academy of Arts and Sciences into ensuring that 'our language' was 'well settled'. In 1821, John Quincy Adams was elected president of a movement with aims very similar to those of his father forty years earlier: it was the American Academy of Language and Belles Lettres. But there was no brash separatism about this organization with its sophisticated articles drafted under the care of its effective leader, W. S. Cardell. It would 'promote the purity and uniformity of the English language' in close collaboration with 'distinguished scholars in other countries speaking this language in common with ourselves'. Outside the discreet formulation of the Articles this was frankly acknowledged (as in a letter from Cardell to the aged Thomas Jefferson, February 1820), as meaning the need to have agreement 'between the British and ourselves', to which end 'a respectful communication' would be sent to 'literary gentlemen in the British dominions . . . inviting their co-operation'.

In this respect, however, the Academy of Language was a hornet's nest. George McDuffie, later governor of South Carolina, was by no means alone among the powerful influences who would have sought to inject it with a more brutally nationalistic purpose ('Shall we wait for the sanction of the British tribunals of criticism, before . . . introducing a new word?'), and in the same year, 1821, Governor T. B. Robertson of Louisiana felt that 'to form an American language' should not be excluded from the Academy's goals. A century later (1923), W. J. McCormick introduced a bill into Congress with just such an uncompromising purpose, 'To define the national and official language of the Government and people of the United States', thereby achieving a 'mental emancipation' from Britain to 'supplement the political emancipation of '76' and make American writers 'drop their top-coats, spats, and swagger-sticks'.

Such radical proposals however received no more official endorsement than the numerous more modest and limited ones that were made throughout this whole period. Although, as a young man, Noah Webster was in agreement with ideas (1786) of promoting linguistic reforms by congressional action, he later (1817, 1820) turned firmly against the academy principle in favour of allowing the democratic process its head: general custom and habit would better direct the language's future. In this, he was of course in tune with the great weight of scholarly opinion.

But however naive the academy movements were and however much the jealous anti-federalist and 'states' rights' sentiments precluded any chance of their success, they reflected and provided a platform for a good deal of eager republicanism which sought linguistic ammunition to promote feelings of identity, loyalty, national pride. In his *Cadmus* of 1793 (for which he was awarded the Philosophical Society's gold medal), William Thornton flamboyantly forecast that 'The AMERICAN LANGUAGE will . . . be as distinct as the government' and many of his contemporaries felt (with 'Sylvius' in the *American Museum*, August 1787) that they had 'the misfortune of speaking the same language with a nation who, of all people in Europe, have given . . . us fewest proofs of love'. In an effort to get round this and to force language to be an emblem of the new nation, it was not uncommon as early as 1780 to refer to oneself as 'speaking American'. So we are told by the Marquis de Chastellux who was repeatedly assured (1780–82) that 'American is not difficult to learn'.

Webster in his earlier writings enthusiastically advocated large-scale spelling changes in order to stimulate the divergence of

American English so that it would become 'a band of national union' (*Dissertations*, 1789). Hence proceed the *-or* and *-er* spellings in *humor*, *center*, etc, though many of his more radical ideas (*bred*, *tuf*, *tung*, *thum*, *iland*, *wimmen*) he later abandoned. Nor was it merely a matter of spelling: in *deef*, *heered*, *cag*, and the like, he was picking on forms which represented one of the current pronunciations in America and which if generalized by being given educational and lexicographical authority would promote and hasten distinctions from British English in speech as well as writing. With *lieutenant* and *schedule*, he actually seems to have succeeded; for the rest, it was perhaps the 'low' associations of his preferred forms that earned them a cool reception by the pace-setters in American linguistic fashion.

With the passing of the years, Webster came to believe strongly in the future of a united Anglo-American English, but his earlier views continued in favour with many outspoken patriots. We have already heard the voices of McDuffie and Robertson in 1821, but in the same year the more judicious tones of Thomas Jefferson were in harmony with them: 'There are so many differences between us and England . . . that we must be left far behind the march of circumstances, were we to hold ourselves rigorously to their standard'. As American self-confidence increased, it was natural to see the American branch of the English language as the more important, with a wider richer vocabulary to match the country's might in both technology and thought. As Walt Whitman put it around 1855 (in *An American Primer*):

> The Americans are going to be the most fluent and melodious voiced people in the world—and the most perfect users of words.—Words follow character—nativity, independence, individuality... These States are rapidly supplying themselves with new words, called for by new occasions, new facts, new politics, new combinations.—Far plentier additions will be needed, and, of course, will be supplied. . .
>
> American writers are to show far more freedom in the use of words. —Ten thousand native idiomatic words are growing, or are to-day already grown, out of which vast numbers could be used by American writers, with meaning and effect—words that would be welcomed by the nation, being of the national blood—words that give that taste of identity and locality which is so dear in literature.

The fluent volubility (in contrast to the inhibited gauchery of British discourse) was acknowledged proudly by an American statesman witnessing the London ambassador in operation. John Hay wrote a letter in 1894 exclaiming, 'How our Ambassador does go it when he gets a roomful of bovine Britons in front of him . . . I never so clearly appreciated the power of the unhesitating orotundity of the Yankee speech, as in listening—after an hour or two of hum-ha of tongue-tied British men—to the long wash of our Ambassador's sonority'.

A typical peak of confidence is found in the critic G. B. Munson who wrote in 1929 of 'carrying the English language ... into a more perfect stage which we may hope will be called American' and which 'could surpass modern English as that surpasses middle English' (*Saturday Review of Literature*). The existence, the popularity, and above all perhaps the title of H. L. Mencken's great book reflect just such an aspiration.

NOTE

1. I have frequently been guided to the early source materials used in this chapter and the next by several invaluable papers distilling the researches of Allen Walker Read: 'British Recognition of American Speech in the Eighteenth Century', *Dialect Notes 6* (1933); 'Amphi-Atlantic English', *English Studies* 17 (1935); 'American Projects for an Academy to Regulate Speech', *PMLA* 51 (1936); 'Suggestions for an Academy in England in the Latter Half of the Eighteenth Century', *Mod. Phil.* 36 (1938); 'The Assimilation of the Speech of British Immigrants in Colonial America', *JEGP* 37 (1938); 'A Dictionary of the English of England: Problems and Findings' (mimeo, 1968). No-one writing on this subject could be without an equally pervasive debt, beyond the scope of specific references, to H. L. Mencken's *The American Language*, especially as edited by R. I. McDavid, Jr (New York, 1963) and made the more indispensable by richness of allusion to modern source work by H. Kurath, A. H. Marckwardt and others. Linguistic developments in Britain since 1776 are given a recent authoritative summary by B. M. H. Strang in *The History of English* (London, 1970), and the contemporary American influence on British English is well treated in B. Foster, *The Changing English Language* (London, 1968), especially Chapter 1.

2 Linguistic Bonds Across the Atlantic

The spirit of *vive la différence* discussed in Chapter 1 was not confined to the western side in the Anglo-American dialogue. Indeed the spotting of differences started as a British colonial-baiting game, has remained a predominantly British prerogative, and for the most part has retained a spiteful, contemptuous flavour. One might almost say that the republican excesses that we have noticed were primarily a defensive reaction.

And the British began as they were to go on: different equals worse. Forty years before the War of Independence, Francis Moore remarked on the use of *bluff* for a steep bank and called it 'barbarous English'.[1] While it is only fair to remind ourselves that many—if not most—British reactions to American English from the eighteenth century have been friendly and favourable, it is the sniping ones that have set the tone. Dr Johnson (in a review of 1756 attributed to him by Boswell) referred to 'the American dialect' as representing 'a tract [i.e. process] of corruption' and in 1760 we find Benjamin Franklin bowing deferentially before the criticisms of David Hume who appears to have disliked (as Americanisms—though with little justification) his using *pejorate*, *colonize*, and *unshakeable*.

If serious writers on serious topics could seem deviant, how much more so the oral folk-speech? A British traveller in 1792, Patrick Campbell, represented an encounter as follows:

> I asked him if he had come from the head of the Lake; he answered in a twang peculiar to the New Englanders, 'I viow niew you may depen I's just a-comin;' 'And what distance may it be from hence?' said I; 'I viow niew I guess I do' no,—I guess niew I do' no,—I swear niew I guess it is three miles;' he swore, vowed, and guessed alternately, and was never like to come to the point, though he had but that instant come from it.

The British stereotype of American speech began to form quite early, in fact. Jonathan Boucher observed 'a slow, drawling' manner 'in American elocution' before 1775, Thomas Twining reported the 'vulgar' pronunciation *fortn* for 'fortune' in 1796, and numerous writers around 1800 commented on the tendency for speech to be bombastic and exaggerated, peppered with superlatives and newfangled words like *locate*, *belittle* (Thomas Jefferson was castigated for this in 1787), *lengthy*, *demoralizing*, *influential*, and others that have equally lost any heinous flavour they possessed: *loan* and *advocate* as verbs, the use of *forks* as 'their manner of describing the partings in the roads'. We have already glimpsed the development of the stereotype in *Martin Chuzzlewit*; ten years earlier, T. P. Thompson had felt that no-one should be 'excused for calling Territory "Terry Tory" '.

Not of course that many people in Britain would have recognized an American by his speech: experience precluded it. A Scot with a somewhat Anglicized pronunciation was taken for an American by a London shopkeeper, Boswell tells us, simply because he spoke something different from either Scots or English, 'which I conclude is the language of America' (*Life of Johnson* II.160).[2] But the accumulation of travellers' tales was leading Englishmen to believe that American speech was strange and uncouth, so that tactless and absurdly inappropriate comments were often forthcoming when an American was heard for the first time. A. W. Read in *English Studies* 17 tells us of how Dr Johnson was rightly rebuked in 1788 for asking a young American in some surprise where he had learnt his good English. In 1815, a cultivated Bostonian reported than an Englishman had 'expressed to me his surprise that I spoke so good English ... This is the first instance I have yet met of this kind of ignorance. He is himself a cockney.' Later in the century, a British army officer took it upon himself to ask a girl from the cream of New England society whether she was not, for an American, exceptionally well spoken, a gaffe which earned the devastating reply, 'Oh yes, but then I had unusual advantages. There was an English missionary stationed near my tribe.'

In print, too, one forms the clear impression that it was enough merely to know that a piece of work was by an American to set critics looking for objectionable language. In which case it was easy to find it and even to affect uncomprehension. In 1803, it was claimed in the *Monthly Magazine* that 'One third of the American Newspapers ... is filled with uncouth advertisements, written, in general, in language ... wholly unintelligible to the English reader'. Or consider the symptomatic attack on American English in the *Edinburgh Review* of October 1809. The occasion was a review of Joel Barlow's enormous epic, *The Columbiad*, published in Philadelphia in 1807 with a London reprint in 1809. However much we may agree with the reviewer that the style is 'cumbrous and inflated . . . with a sort of turbulent and bombastic elevation', for literally hundreds of pages, and however stridently the poet seeks to glorify America, it is in no obvious way written in typically American English. Indeed the 1807 version, protracting and embellishing an already long and ornate poem of twenty years earlier (*The Vision of Columbus*), too obviously reflects the poet's many years of work and study in England and France, absorbing still more of the traditional image machinery and epic pastiche that were already endemic in *The Vision*.

Yet the reviewer seizes the occasion to identify the language and style with the subject and to scour the copious material for evidence to prove that Barlow is writing

in a language utterly unknown to the prose or verse of this country. We have often heard it reported, that our transatlantic brethren were beginning to take it amiss that their language should still be called English; and truly we must say, that Mr Barlow has gone far to take away that ground of reproach. The groundwork of his speech, perhaps, may be English, as that of the Italian is Latin; but the variations amount already to more than a change of dialect; and really make a glossary necessary for most untravelled readers. As this is the first specimen which has come to our hands of any considerable work composed in the American tongue, it may be gratifying to our philological readers, if we make a few remarks upon it.

It is distinguished from the original English, in the first place, by a great multitude of words which are radically and entirely new, and as utterly foreign as if they had been adopted from the Hebrew or Chinese; in the second place, by a variety of new compounds and combinations of words, or roots of words, which are still known in the parent tongue; and, thirdly, by the perversion of a still greater number of original English words from their proper use or signification, by employing nouns substantive for verbs, for instance, and adjectives for substantives, &c. We shall set down a few examples of each.

In the first class, we may reckon the words *multifluvian—cosmogyral—crass—role—gride—conglaciate—colon* and *coloniarch—trist* and *contristed—thirl—gerb—ludibrious—croupe—scow—emban—lowe—brume—brumal*, &c. &c.

The second class is still more extensive, and, to our ears, still more discordant. In it we may comprehend such verbs as, to *utilise*, to *vagrate*, to *oversheet*, to *empalm*, to *inhumanise*, to *transboard*, to *reseek*, to *bestorm*, to *ameed*, &c. &c.; such adjectives as *bivaulted, imbeaded, unkeeled, laxed, forestered, homicidious, millennial, portless, undungeoned, lustred*, &c——*conflicting fulminents;* and a variety of substantives formed upon the same plan of distortion.

The third or last class of American improvements, consists mainly in the violent transformation of an incredible number of English nouns into verbs. Thus we have, 'to *spade* the soil'—'to *sledge* the corn'—

and 'to *keel* the water.' We have also the verbs, to *breeze*, to *rainbow*, to *hill*, to *scope*, to *lot*, to *lamp*, to *road*, and to *reroad*, to *fang*, to *fray*, to *bluff*, to *tone*, to *forester*, to *gyve*, to *besom*, and fifty more. Nor is it merely as verbs that our poor nouns are compelled to serve in this new republican dictionary; they are forced, upon a pinch, to do the duty of adjectives also; and, accordingly, we have science distinguished into moral science and *physic* science; and *things* discussed with a view to their *physic* forms and their final ends.

Just as we have seen American nationalism colouring linguistic attitudes, so political antipathy to America coloured the British attitude to American English. So despicable a country was developing a language to match. A Dean of Canterbury, Henry Alford, made a *Plea for the Queen's English* in 1863 when he invited his readers to consider the 'deterioration' it was suffering in America and explicitly compared the Americans' moral deterioration ('Look at those phrases . . . and then compare the character and history of the nation—its blunted sense of moral obligation and duty to man'), instancing—somewhat to our surprise today—the current war against the slave-owning confederacy.

On this view, of course, it was not just a matter of *noticing* differences between the two 'languages' but of being thankful for the differences. America 'must develop her own language and allow us to develop ours', said a writer in the *New Statesman* (June 1927); indeed, already he felt 'The American language is the American language and the English language is the English language'. In full agreement, another writer in this journal (February 1928) claimed that 'many people . . . would like to see the English and American languages as independent of one another as French and Italian'. This was not far from the view of even so scholarly and urbane a man as J. R. R. Tolkien: 'Whatever be the special destiny and peculiar future splendour of the language of the United States, it is still possible to hope that our fate may be kept distinct' (*Year's Work in English Studies*, 1925).

This meant that our energies must be directed to keeping the English of Britain pure from trans-Atlantic pollution, even if driven to invoking some kind of official control. For while attention has been drawn above to post-revolutionary moves in America for a language 'Academy', it must not be thought that there had been no analogous ideas in Britain during this period. Swift's goals continued in fact to have select but distinguished support. George Harris in 1752 advocated a spelling reform backed by parliamentary authority. Robert Baker appealed to George III in 1770 to set up an Academy in order to regulate good use and to rid English of 'Incorrectnesses and Barbarisms'.

Robert Nares set forth a similar proposal in 1781, and in 1788, when the New York Philological Society was being formed for 'ascertaining and improving the *American Tongue*', an appeal was made in the *Gentleman's Magazine* that Herbert Croft should organize a means to 'remedy all such defects as our language may contain'.

One British proposal was far more radical (and ridiculous) than anything that was formulated by the republican enthusiasts of New York. John Pinkerton, writing as Robert Heron (*Letters of Literature*, 1785), hoped that the king would appoint one hundred ('or indeed all') learned men to constitute the Academy for Improving the Language, with a regularized grammar in which all adjectives would agree with nouns in a number inflexion; a modified phonology which would tend to prevent words from ending in 'harsh consonants'; and a partially reformed orthography. A specimen:

> I cast mina eyea towardo the summito of a roco, tha waz noto faro fro me

It was not part of Pinkerton's eccentric aim to distinguish by this means the language of Britain from that of America. In fact, most of these early British proposals paid no specific attention to the trans-Atlantic issue. One of the rare exceptions was that of Herbert Croft. Planning to supersede Johnson's dictionary, he described his projected 'Oxford English Dictionary' in the *Gentleman's Magazine* in 1788 a few months before the appeal was made to him in the same columns to help remedy the deficiencies of English. In making his dictionary, he wrote, 'America and American books will not be neglected . . . The American ambassador has taken charge of some letters . . . which will, no doubt, produce communications from the other side of the Atlantick'. The ambassador in question was the future President, John Adams, who was doubtless still interested in promoting his own proposal of 1780 for an American Academy (see above, p. 10). It was doubtless through his relations with Adams (and Thomas Jefferson, who also corresponded with him) that Croft came to see the importance of Anglo-American co-operation in this field, and in his *Letter . . . to the Princess Royal . . . on the English and German languages* (1797) he shows an extraordinary breadth of vision:

> The future history of the other three quarters of the world will, probably, be much affected by America's speaking the language of England . . . Perhaps we are, just now, not very far distant from the precise moment, for making some grand attempt, with regard to

fixing the *standard* of our language . . . in America. Such an attempt would, I think, succeed in America, for the same reasons that would make it fail in England . . .

Among other equally abortive suggestions to standardize English by authority, there was one in the late nineteenth century that involved seeking American co-operation. In his book on *The Past, Present and Future of England's languages* (1878), W. Marshall appealed 'to the citizens of the United States, for, despite laws and constitutions, they and we are brothers, and equal sharers in one literature', to participate in an academy which would be 'composed of scholars elected from England, from the United States, and from our colonies'. A more recent example is the careful system of simplified English invented by C. K. Ogden, and characteristically given a name which is an acronymic pun, 'Basic'—British American Scientific International Commercial, reflecting Ogden's reasonable conviction that no such grand design was thinkable without Anglo-American co-operation.

But for the most part, calls for the regulation of 'England's Language' (and let us never forget that they were always rare, unrepresentative, and tangential to most contemporary thought), have either ignored America or (in the present century) been characterized by an obsession to protect English from Americanization. There was something of a climax in the late nineteen twenties, partly as a reaction to an International Conference on English held in Bloomsbury in 1927, and partly under the onslaught of the Hollywood sound-track from 1929. Hysteria on the latter ground is not perhaps surprising: to those who either disliked America or were liable in any case to see standards of English declining, the 'talkie' was a towering threat. Even the subtitles on silent films were damaging enough, with their slangy brevity thrust before the eyes of admiring, impressionable young folk. Within a few months of the 'talkie', an MP demanded an embargo on such American imports by the Board of Trade in order to 'protect the English language' (4 February 1930) and told the press that 'there can be no doubt that such films are an evil influence on our language', considering that in Britain alone 'thirty million people visit the cinemas every week. What is the use of spending millions on education if our young people listen to falsified English spoken every night?'

But it was less to be expected—and more to be deplored—that angry and ignorant outbursts should have greeted a small gathering of distinguished people meeting under the auspices of the Royal Society of Literature and in the interests of 'maintaining the traditions and fostering the development of our common tongue'. We might not have expected the ordinary sensation-hungry reporter to realize the eminence of the American delegates —J. L. Lowes, G. P. Krapp, Kemp Malone (though they happened to include Britain's great lexicographer William A. Craigie, who was knighted the following year). But one would have thought that adequate reassurance would have been provided by the names of the British delegates: for example, Lord Balfour, a former Conservative Prime Minister; Sir John Reith, head of the BBC; Sir Israel Gollancz, the Secretary of the British Academy. Yet while *The Times* was merely cool and sceptical and the *Spectator* actually sympathetic, a long and vicious tirade in the *New Statesman* (June 1927)stirred up the worst suspicions and bitterest jingoism. English is 'our language'—where *our* does not refer even to the British as a whole but to 'the people who dwell south of Hadrian's Wall' and who were in consequent danger of being under-represented. 'We cannot treat the question on Imperial lines. The Canadians have adopted most of the vulgarisms of the United States. The Australians have their own semi-American patois'. Neither these nor (above all) the Americans should have any say in deciding what is good English. 'Their choice is to accept our authority or else make their own language'.

It would be comforting to think that such benighted naivety would be impossible in the contracted world of a more recent generation, but on 4 July 1955 a letter in the London *Daily Telegraph* ended with just such an empty, parochial, nonsensical gesture: 'If other nations wish to borrow or adopt our language, it is up to them, but let it be understood that the language remains fundamentally ours'. The irony of such a letter on the 4th of July would probably have escaped the writer, but of him it could be said as Kemp Malone said of the *New Statesman* protagonist of 1927, 'had he been born in America, [he] would have made an excellent mayor of Chicago' (*American Speech* 3.272).

What seems to have especially wounded those with misplaced national pride was the report that one of the American delegates, Dr H. S. Canby, had alluded to features specific to British usage as 'Anglicisms'. This further sign that Americans might claim 'a right equal to our own to decide what is English' was the last straw for the *New Statesman* commentator. He became as petulant as a spoilt child who wants the beach to himself. 'The English language is our own, and we may do what we please with it, and we cannot submit to any sort of foreign dictation' and so we 'obviously cannot admit' that it 'contains "Anglicisms" '.

There were weightier reasons than nonsense of this sort militating against official Anglo-American co-operation to regulate English, and although a modest programme was drafted by the

British scholar, J. H. G. Grattan, the International Council of English was as abortive as earlier 'Academies' had been, on either side of the Atlantic.

It is ironic that Canby's clinical reference to 'Anglicisms' should have caused such fury. Stung by sneers like those in the *Edinburgh Review* of October 1809, Americans had rather naturally been reacting spiritedly since the early years of the Republic. Indeed it was in 1809 that a fictitious account of *The Yankee in London* scored a point against British comments on 'I guess' and the like by jibing at British colloquial use of *clever* and *fellow*. In 1817 Webster wrote to John Pickering: 'I can furnish as long a catalogue of the changes introduced into England, as any Englishman can of *our* deviations'. J. L. Kingsley of Yale claimed (1829: *North American Review*) that the English press was running riot with neologism paying far less attention to 'the authority of good writers, and to the decision of lexicographers' than was the case in America. Of the many words that had been brought into recent British use, 'most of which are wholly unnecessary', he gave such examples as *absenteeism, dupery, ill-timed, metapolitics*. With the first of these he displays a particularly sharp eye since (according to the *OED*) it was first recorded only three months before his comment. But some of the others (notably *ill-timed*) are no more valid than the many 'Americanisms' that have been condemned by British critics in ignorance of their actual origin in British use.

In addition to keeping their end up to the extent of saying 'Tu quoque: your neologisms are at least as bad as ours', some Americans have also turned the tables in seeking to protect the purity of American English against insidious infiltration westward across the Atlantic. Manuals encouraged writers to use their natural, authentic, home-bred language, and warned them against sycophantic aping of London styles, importing British expressions or pronunciations, and any other deviation from a right-thinking indigenous basis of imitation. This doubtless tended to mitigate what Mencken calls the 'Anglomania', the oedipal yearning for the Mother Country which afflicts a substantial number of Americans, generation after generation. A writer in the *New York Review* (April 1842) advised as follows: 'Equally careful should we be to preserve our independence of any illicit fashions of speech which chanced to be in use in England. Otherwise we may be importing affectations, and vulgarisms, and provincialisms . . .' After all, if someone indulges in an affectation, how is he to know whether it is merely, 'in this country, a copy of a second-rate British affectation'? (Richard Grant White, *Words and Their Uses*, 1870). Frequently, however, such relatively inaccessible advice could have little effect. One example: in the

Goodrich-Webster of 1843, *nasty* still has only the 'strong' meanings. By 1870, White is inveighing against the use of the figurative sense, 'disagreeable', as an unwanted Briticism. Albert Rhodes included it with *bloody* and *beastly* as undesirable Briticisms in 1872 (*Galaxy*) and T. W. Higginson linked it with *beastly* as affectation from England to be avoided as 'repulsive' (*Harpers Bazaar*, 1893). But *nasty* established itself firmly in American use for all that.

Such prescriptive efforts continue sporadically: *aren't I* is the target of numerous critics, and in more than one of his handbooks John Opdycke has flatly condemned both *ain't I* and *aren't I* in speech or writing as 'corrupt forms', the latter having the additional grounds for anathema that it is 'a British colloquialism' which 'is not correct and is used in [the United States] for affectation only' (*Get it Right*, New York 1935, p. 179).

On the whole, however, Americans have shown little fear of Briticisms, doubtless in part because there has not been much danger of them but in part also because Briticisms have not had the aura of barbarism for Americans that Americanisms have had for many British people. This is not to say that a British flavour is generally found pleasurable. In many respects it is not. British pronunciation (especially 'RP') seems to the average American clipped, cold and rather effeminate while many British colloquial expressions 'somehow set his teeth on edge', as Mencken puts it. Good-tempered amusement is probably the most widespread reaction by the less experienced and less educated masses, for whom a well established (if not well informed) stereotype of British speech has evolved over the last century and a half. As Anthony Trollope's mother showed in her *Domestic Manners of the Americans*, the image was virtually complete by about 1830. Like the British stereotype of American English, which does not easily distinguish gangster slang from the Senate speech of an elder statesman, the American tends to lump together the Cockney *h*-dropping, archaic *h*-addition, Midland plosives after velar nasals (*anythink*), flapper-age Woosterisms (*Top hole!*), and early Victorian Wellerisms (*werry*). In addition, however, there are more interesting attempts to capture in spelling some of the features of RP as they strike the American ear: 'A fwightfully Bwitish lawt of cheps'.

It is well that we have concluded this section on linguistic antipathies with such light-hearted examples. Teasing without bitterness indeed far more generally characterizes the awareness of each other's speech throughout the whole period than the gloomy pomposity or barbed spite that we have perhaps over-illustrated. The typical level is illustrated by the gag-line in *My*

Fair Lady, 'In America they haven't spoken it for years' and in the New York burlesque *My Square Lady* with its song, 'What makes the Limey talk so square?' The weight of responsible and authoritative opinion on both sides has always been thoroughly practical: seeing a genuinely common language and seizing the advantages that lay in this. Such opinion has always sensibly tended away from separatism and despite great divergencies in educational, social and political institutions has looked for ways of sharing dictionaries, grammars, scientific documentation, and of course literature (including, especially latterly, oral and filmed works).

Even in Britain, where attitudes were always cooler, there are voices from the eighteenth to the twentieth century not only recognizing the unity of the two branches of English but raised strongly in favour of preserving and enhancing that unity. For example, in his *Letter . . . to the Princess Royal* of 1797, Croft glories in the fact that English is the language both of Britain and the United States and adds: 'Deservedly immortal would be that patriot, on either side of the Atlantick, who should succeed' in fixing for all time a unified standard for this widespread tongue; and in 1918 we find Sir Walter Raleigh acclaiming 'the triumph of our common language and our common ideals'. The rhetoric of this must not disguise the fact that is accurately implied by Raleigh. The aims that abortive academies (such as the American Academy of Language, 1820: see above, p. 10) wrote into their optimistic proposals have been substantially realized in the natural course of things by the due process of political and social history.

To a very considerable extent this is due to the linguistic momentum of colonial rule which seems to have perpetuated a bedrock of London orientation in the new republic right through the generations of bitter assertiveness to a period when modern communications were able to offset the divisive influences of nationalism and separate development. There is plenty of good evidence to support even so sweeping a generalization.

First, some pre-revolution indications that the British capital constituted the standard of English in the American colonies throughout the seventeenth and eighteenth centuries. When English was first taken to the United States, nearly everyone pronounced the *r* in words like *bird*. London and other eastern districts of England lost the *r* and it seems unlikely to be coincidence that two important social centres in colonial America (broadly, Boston, Massachusetts and Charleston, South Carolina) should have lost the *r* too. Again, both in Britain and America during the seventeenth century words like *meat* and *loin* were pronounced rather like *mate* and *line* respectively. Yet on both sides of the Atlantic, almost everyone who has been within ear-shot of a schoolteacher has adopted what is the universal standard English form of these words. The exceptions seem to press the point home: people in Ireland, the Isle of Man and the Tennessee valley are among those still heard saying 'jiner' and such like. Their forebears would also seem to have had in common a relative remoteness from (or lack of interest in) the corridors of linguistic power two hundred years ago.

An interesting source of evidence is presented in eighteenth-century press advertisements seeking the recovery of runaway servants. Personal traits offered to assist identification often included the impression they would give from their speech.:

Run away ... a convict servant man, named *William Springate* ... bred in Bristol, and speaks in that dialect.

This appeared in the *Pennsylvania Gazette*, in 1771, and is characteristic of the expectation that Americans on the eve of the republic knew what the Bristol dialect, 3000 miles away, sounded like. They were expected to carry round a recognition knowledge of other dialects as well: Scots, Irish, Welsh (which English speakers are still expected to have, from Alaska to Tasmania); West country, North country, Yorkshire, Cheshire, Manchester ... This shows the extent of British orientation. But the advertisements covertly demonstrate something much more important. They do *not* normally offer London or the dialects of the English home counties as identifying features, any more than they waste money and space to say that the servant speaks with an American accent. London tacitly constitutes a (literally) 'unmarked' norm against which other dialects are contrasted. When London is mentioned it is only as explanation of the good English (that is, the decent 'standard' English) that the wanted person uses. For example (and this is again from the *Pennsylvania Gazette* in 1771):

Run away ... an Irish servant man ... by trade a baker ... He speaks very good English, he having lived near ten years in London.

It was against this unquestioning assumption of a London stan-dard that the linguistic nationalists of the new republic had to fight, and it was a battle that they could not hope to win easily or quickly. Webster's complaint in the *Dissertations* of 1789 that Americans still had 'astonishing respect for the arts and literature of their parent country, and a blind imitation of its manners' was to be vainly repeated for several generations. By James Russell Lowell, for example, in *A Fable for Critics* (1848):

You steal Englishmen's books and think Englishmen's thought;
With their salt on her tail your wild eagle is caught;
Your literature suits its each whisper and motion
To what will be thought of it over the ocean.

W. S. Cardell, the energy behind the American Academy of Language, betrays his anxious conservatism in a letter of 1821 explaining how he saw the Academy working. Lists of words to be discouraged or encouraged or explained would be compiled. 'Without any dogmatical exercise of authority, if such words as "lengthy", "to tote", and "to approbate", should be published as doubtful or bad, they would generally fall into disuse'. He thus picked as examples three of the words that had been most subject to British criticism as barbarous Americanisms, and thereby clearly indicated where he placed the canons of good use.

Political independence was far from being matched by linguistic independence, and the Philadelphia journal *Port Folio* attacked the linguistic nationalists in 1801, sarcastically equating the 'American Tongue' with the speech of the lowest classes: 'to *clip the king's English* is an "unalienable" privilege, adhesive to every *freeborn* boozer, from the clamorous circle of a July feast, down to *citizen* Sambo, who tipples alone'.

Fifty years later and Washington Irving is lending his prestige also to the recognition of a supreme London standard. In a letter to the Merriam Company, he wrote that, whatever is done to improve the English of America, 'yet the world will look to London as the standard of pure English' and 'Any deviation on our part from the best London usage will be liable to be considered as a provincialism'. Again, C. A. Bristed in an essay of 1855 on 'The English Language in America': 'the actual usage of educated Englishmen must be the standard of English'. So too in Richard Grant White's oracular guidance of the last quarter of the nineteenth century. And it is an attitude that was by no means dead even after fifty years of powerful counter-indoctrination from Mencken's *The American Language*. In the spring of 1971, I received an engraved card from a friend in Charlottesville, Virginia, on which it stated that he had 'the honour of announcing the marriage of his daughter'. By what convention is the long-established American spelling of *honor* replaced on such an occasion?

It is an attitude which, however unworthily motivated in some who held it, played an invaluable part in preserving Anglo-American linguistic unity. Indeed, by the time the ease and rapidity of modern communication was ready to step in and prevent fissiparous development, the centre of influence was interestingly shifting from the east side of the Atlantic to the west. Increasingly during the present century, American English has come to have the fashionable prestige in Britain (and other Commonwealth countries), especially with the young, that British English has traditionally had, especially perhaps with the elderly, in the United States.

The net result is that there has been little divergence of British and American English. Many of the indubitable linguistic differences between a given American and a given Briton are individual differences, social differences, or differences that reflect dialect variation within one or other community: they often do not, in other words, reflect differences between British and American English as such. Even where there are differences at the national level, it is the degree of complex overlap that is striking. The 'American' *automobile* is rare in Britain, but *car* is general and in no way 'British' in America. Despite American *faucet* versus British *tap*, Americans drink *tapwater*, and in several areas prefer *spigot* or (especially in Canada) *tap* to *faucet*: just as *faucet* and *spigot* are used in several British dialects in preference to *tap* or (more widely) for special kinds of tap. *Sick* and *ill*: but many Britons feel that *ill* is slightly precious and even those who do not are able to use *sick* with its American generality in nouns such as *sickness* and in the military parlance of 'reporting sick'. *Mad* and *angry*: but in America this use of *mad* is chiefly colloquial and in several British dialects it is used in precisely the same way. *Sidewalk* and *pavement* are more nearly Anglo-American differences, though *pavement* has the 'British' meaning in Philadelphia and is replaced by *sidewalk* in some British use, while Liverpool Corporation uses *pavement* in the 'American' sense.

Mail and *post* are interesting examples of the complexity that is possible. While Americans handle their mail (or post)—which may include *post*cards—through the *post* office and the *postal* services with *postage* stamps, the British deal with the post (or mail) with the help of *mail*bags in *mail* vans, *mail* trains, *Royal Mail* steamers, and there is the air *mail* service. Yet although Americans sometimes speak of the *postman* delivering their letters, there is no corresponding British use of *mailman*.

So we could go on. The long and imposing lists of so-called distinctively British and American words and usages that are found in hand-books are highly misleading: both the items so neatly separated are either well-known in one or other country or, as frequently is the case, in both. At best, these lists draw attention to a difference in preferred usage on either side of the Atlantic, a particular word or one sense of a word being in minority or specialized use in the other community. For example, both *pig* and *hog* occur in both British and American use, but in Britain *pig* is the general word, with *hog* being either specialized or metaphorical, while in America *hog* is the general word, *pig* being specialized (newly born) or metaphorical. The pairs *yours sincerely* and *sincerely yours*, *dessert* and *sweet* also have a complex if less interesting distribution. One can *bathe* in the sea in both communities but only Americans can do so in a bath (tub); *bath* as a transitive verb is used similarly by the Americans and British but intransitively it does for the British a good deal of what is expressed by *bathe* for Americans. The word *academic* tends to be neutral as between arts and science in Britain but to be weighted in the arts direction when Americans use it.

In many cases the strangest apparent differences show cases of where the Americans have perpetuated in standard use a once universal word now replaced in British standard usage but surviving in the dialects. The American use of 'I guess' was frequent in early English writers such as Chaucer; *homely* in the American sense of 'plain, unattractive' was used by Shakespeare and Milton in that sense too, though today 'a homely girl' could certainly be misunderstood in Anglo-American discourse.

Most instances one hears or reads of failures in British and American communication, however, are carefully engineered examples of where an observer (or wit) thinks misunderstanding might be possible. For example, a widely publicized difference between American and British usage concerns interrogative forms of *have*-sentences. In American English, the auxiliary *do* is normally used: 'Do you have enough money?' In much British English, *do* tends to be confined to contexts of habitual action: 'Do you (normally) have eggs for breakfast?' This observation is made to support the anecdote of an American asking an English woman 'Do you have many children?' and getting the answer, 'Oh no, only one every couple of years'.

Misunderstandings of this sort are however scarcely possible in real life, partly because the distinction in usage is not so absolute as some writers would have us believe, and partly because even where for a given pair of speakers the distinction in usage is absolute, it is widely known that the other construction exists and allowance is readily made for variant interpretations when it occurs. So too, although no American uses *public school* in the sense 'special type of private school', and British people would hardly use *public school* in the American sense of 'state school', misunderstanding can scarcely arise because the British peculiarity is well known in America, and because the American equivalent 'private school' or 'preparatory school' is unlikely to cause difficulty to an Englishman.

None of this must be allowed to obscure the very real differences that inevitably sprang up as English established itself in the transatlantic setting. The earliest English settlers in the New World found many new features and experiences for which they had no names. They coined new ones like *mocking bird, rattlesnake, eggplant* or gave familiar names from Old England to similar but unrelated objects in New England—*robin* for the red-breasted thrush, for instance, and *corn* for the new common grain, maize. Or they adopted words from the Indian natives—*hickory, squash, moccasin* and possibly *caucus*—or from earlier French settlers to the north of them (*prairie, chowder*), or from the New Amsterdam Dutch (*coleslaw, cookie, boss*, and probably *Yankee* itself, from *Jan Kees*, a common nickname for the Dutch which came to be applied to New Englanders as well). Later on, English-speaking Americans also adopted words from the German settlers in Pennsylvania, though most of these adoptions have remained dialectal in farming communities (*thick milk* 'curdled milk', G. *Dickmilch, smearcase* 'cottage cheese', G. *Schmierkäse*), but probably the widely known expression *dumb cluck* is from Pennsylvania Germans' use of *Klucke* 'a sitting hen', and the frequent use by Americans of a verb *dunk*, used of dipping doughnuts into coffee, is certainly the German *dunken* 'dip'.

But it was during the nineteenth century that independent developments in the two main branches of English proliferated. This follows naturally from several factors. There was political as well as (increasingly) social and artistic independence, with separatist tendencies unmitigated by the ease and rapidity of twentieth-century communications and by the fresh intimacy in political and social relations that we have seen since the First World War. At the same time, the period of relative isolation in the nineteenth century saw rapid expansion of population in the United States together with the immense changes accompanying the industrial revolution (later in America than in Britain) and the rapid technological developments that provided large and separate areas of vocabulary, as we noted earlier (pp. 2–3). But new American expressions that might have puzzled Englishmen towards the end of the Victorian age cover a wide spectrum and are in no way predominantly technical: *cocktail, icebox, gerrymander, the spoils system, bowie knife, goldfever, bloomers, coeducation, rustler, apartment house, nickelodeon, stenographer, gangster, basketball, mortician*. The Englishman would not have connected 'commuting' with public transport or 'splitting a ticket' with politics.

During the same period, British English made equally independent development, and among the words that would have seemed strange to an American towards the end of the nineteenth century, we might mention *bungalow*, *swank*, *flapper* (a girl), *tabloid* (newspaper), *gadget*, (telephone) *exchange*, *hoarding*, *paraffin*, *lorry*, *spanner*, *blackleg*, *braces*, *kipper*, *drawing pin*, *tram(car)*. As with the American list, care has been taken to illustrate the range of vocabulary involved by avoiding concentration on the obvious fields of strictly technological development.

Even during the nineteenth century, however, there was a transatlantic linguistic traffic, some British expressions being imported into America (*nasty*, *swagger*, and several golf terms, for example), but a vastly greater number moving in the opposite direction: *blizzard*, *immigrant*, *snag*, *snow-plough*, *(make a) bee-line*, *bunkum*, political terms like *wirepulling* and *sitting on the fence*, and, among many other examples, general idiomatic phrases such as *strike oil*, *make a pile*, *take a back seat*, *face the music*, *go back on*, *get the hang of*, and of course *O.K.*

But such a traffic was the merest trickle to the flood that has arisen in the twentieth century and particularly since the Second World War when both on a political and on a social level (for the first time in history, it was possible for hundreds of thousands of young men to establish close transatlantic relations) the two countries came increasingly to communicate without even noticing American and British peculiarities. Modern communication techniques have powerfully contributed to the same end. The part played by film, radio, and television (especially important since the advent of Telstar transmission) has been well acknowledged. So has the part played by advertising, especially the advertising by firms marketing goods on a world scale. Less attention has been paid to the teleprinter-assisted news agency though this is perhaps the most fruitful source of Anglo-American linguistic exchange. Not merely do the subeditors processing the English-language news flashes become rapidly blunted in their ability to detect (and so replace) a specific American or British expression: the unedited item in a hundred local papers is accompanied by no unfamiliar voice or context announcing to the Los Angeles reader that this is a Briticism or to the Leeds reader that this is an Americanism. Doubtless through such 'subliminal' teaching, British readers are continually absorbing transatlantic expressions without even knowing them to be of American origin. The adoption of words through films and television is in contrast fairly conscious and even deliberate.

The study of Anglo-American linguistic relations at the present time not merely continues to be of great interest, but is capable still of surprising us. There are three prime sources of surprise. First the sheer energy of the linguistic traffic: its extent, its speed, and—despite the enormous imbalance of power—its continuing two-way nature. During the inter-war years David Low's cartoon character 'Colonel Blimp' (born of a 1916 British word for a dirigible airship) provided a new colloquial word for a pompous reactionary. The word not merely spread from Britain to America in this sense but by the nineteen fifties was being used without as it were any import duty being levied on its British origin: no quotation marks round it, no apologies or explanations, and (in the dictionaries) no 'esp. Brit.'.

Secondly, one is constantly struck by the profoundly intimate and subtle way in which there is agreement between the two branches of the language. The nuances that enable poetry (and indeed humour) to work in both communities give adequate if implicit testimony of this. But for explicit testimony we can turn to the detailed usage notes in the dictionaries and grammars, spelling out the extraordinary unanimity that exists over the bulk of the language. In reading some draft material on one occasion by the American lexicographer C. L. Barnhart, I repeatedly found descriptions like the following, satisfactorily accounting also for British use in respect of features that were by no means obvious: *gent* 'for more than a hundred years, it has had no currency among the educated except as a deliberate imitation of non-standard usage'; *genteel* 'a word of favourable connotation only among those relatively unfamiliar with the standard language; among the educated, when used at all, it is ironical or disparaging'.

Thirdly—and especially in view of the previous two—we can be sharply surprised by the hidden reefs of continuing differences. There are areas of usage where (unlike *talk with* or *aside from*) the British are stubbornly resistant to American influence: they will not adopt 'zee' or '*one* must do *his* best', for example. There are little areas of difference which are virtually unknown since both versions are understood and neither community realizes that constraints exist. For example while in both varieties one can say 'I forgot the key' and 'I forgot to ask her' and while in both 'I omitted the word' is also commonplace, it is largely a British usage to say 'I omitted to remind her'. More importantly, neither community realizes that the British do not really understand the American use of *visit with*. An American who rings up a London acquaintance and asks 'Can you suggest sometime when I can visit with you?' will doubtless be invited to a meal with the Londoner's family, and this seems a satisfactory outcome. But the American (who has meant 'Can we have a talk somewhere, sometime?') would be horrified to realize that the Londoner thinks his acquaintance has invited himself to his home. There are even usages where it is possible for serious misunderstanding to arise: in the sentence, 'The watchman should ring the police *just in case* someone gets in through the window', the complex conjunction in italics could be interpreted as 'only if' in America but as 'lest' in Britain. And the curiously tighter control by the school ma'am produces odd anomalies. The original London edition of Graham Greene's novel, *The End of the Affair* (Heinemann 1951), contains the following two sentences: 'The world would have said he had the reasons for hate, not me' (p. 3). 'She did not believe in anything, anymore than you or me' (p. 166). In the American edition by Bantam Books we find *me* replaced by *I* in each case (pp. 2, 117). Such examples sharply contradict the image of American speech as tough, creative, convention-flouting, and imbued with the virility of the frontier spirit. It is a reminder of the complexities in the British and American varieties of English and a warning against oversimplification.

NOTES

1. See Chapter 1, Note 1.

2. A story of the obverse occurring in the 1920's shows that the 'British remained unable to identify American speech until the very eve of films with sound-track. I owe to my colleague Joel Hurstfield the report of Wallace Notestein asking locals in a Devonshire pub where they thought he came from. They said they had already been discussing this very problem and had come to the conclusion that he was from Yorkshire. This was doubtless not because they thought it matched any north country speech they had actually heard but because Notestein's dialect was so thoroughly exotic that it must hail from somewhere remote from Devon—such as Yorkshire.

3 English Today: A World View

One of the few books I've read on teaching English to speakers of other languages is the first such book I read: Leonard Q. Ross's *The Education of Hyman Kaplan* which was published in 1937 (earlier seriatim in the *New Yorker*). Mr Kaplan, you will recall, was one of the pupils in that wave of home-based TESOL aimed at naturalizing the refugees of the thirties. He was one of 'the thirty-odd adults in the beginners' grade of the American Night Preparatory School for Adults ("English—Americanization—Civics—Preparation for Naturalization")' (p. 7). The book stated the TESOL priorities unambiguously. 'For the students in the beginners' grade, vocabulary was a dire and pressing need. Spelling, after all, was not of such immediate importance to people who did little writing during their daily lives. Grammar? They needed the substance—words, phrases, idioms—to which grammar might be applied. Pronunciation? Mr Parkhill had come to the reluctant conclusion that for some of them accurate pronunciation was a near impossibility. Take Mr Kaplan for example . . . Mr Kaplan, when asked to use "heaven" in a sentence, had replied promptly, "In sommer, ve all heaven a fine time" ' (p. 33). But if this was the first book I read on TESOL, it was by no means the first book I read that touched on the English of immigrants. In *The American Scene* of 1907, we have Henry James's reflections on the customers of central European origin in the Eastside cafés of New York. 'Why,' he asks, 'were the quiet easy couples, with their homely café habit . . . , such remote and indirect results of our local anecdotic past, our famous escape, at our psychological moment, from King George and his works . . . ? Yet why, on the other hand, could they affect one . . . as still more disconnected from the historic consciousness implied in their own type, and with . . . identity . . . too extinct in them for any possibility of renewal?' James goes on to speak of one man's 'fluent Eastside

This was the inauguration paper at the TESOL Convention in Chicago, March 1969.

New Yorkese ... and the colour and the quality of it, and the free familiarity and the "damned foreign impudence," with so much taken for granted'; James muses on the 'inward assimilation of our heritage and point of view' and asks 'What, oh, what again, were he and his going to make of us?' (pp. 206–7).

In recent years, in your country and in mine, teaching English to speakers of other languages has often meant especially teaching inhabitants of other countries—the Philippines, Indonesia, Africa, Thailand, India. But it is not inappropriate that the two references I have made to my early reading in this field should have been to the English of inhabitants of the principal English-speaking country, and I notice with great interest that the programme of this convention reflects a deep concern for the special groups within the United States. And here, it seems to me, is where a world view is relevant. In South Africa, in Australia, in New Zealand, in Britain, in Canada perhaps with peculiar sharpness at this moment, as well as in these United States, the English of orthodox law-enacting, culture-bearing, education-disseminating is in conflict with less orthodox English or with the needs of those whose historic language was not English at all: either because they entered our society long after English became established (like the Pakistanis of Britain or the Latin Americans of the United States); or because their language was current in these areas before ever the English tongue was heard there (like the Welsh of Britain or the Indians of the United States).

The social, political, and educational problems concerned are in their very infancy but this much we can reasonably predict: that all of them are going to require sophisticated linguistic inquiry to underpin the sociological and educational programmes we tentatively frame in this generation and the next.

A session at this convention is going to be devoted to the notion of 'Standard English'—as well it might. How does any form of language have conferred upon it that status of 'standard'? Are the practical factors connected with a standard's role as lingua franca dissociable from the emotional factors connected with a standard's prestige? Do all non-standard varieties of a language have an equal lack of prestige and if not, why not? Are the measures linguistic or sociological? What are the special problems in relation to English?

It seems to me that varieties of performance in a language have three dimensions (see Fig. 1).

The horizontal left-right dimension deals with the *similarities* of the varieties of a language relative to each other, and the other dimensions can be held constant with respect to it. If we have highest adequacy and highest prestige (leaving aside for a moment

what these dimensions imply), it is along this horizontal of similarity that the various 'standard' forms of English belong: notably
American English and British English. These two major standards
are sufficiently close on the similarity dimension to provide no

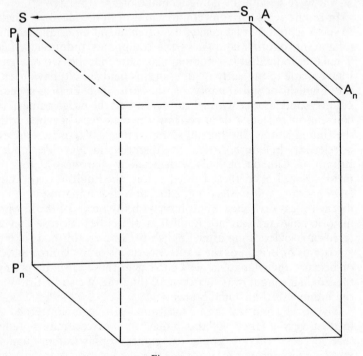

Figure 1
S = Similarity; A = Adequacy; P = Prestige.

serious problems in the TESOL situation, and we all know of
instances throughout the world where American and British
teachers collaborate on the ground, so to speak, with the same
students. For the most part, however, students opt in effect for one
standard or the other according to where they live and the teachers available. The strong preferences sometimes expressed for one
or other variety are normally made on trivial grounds or through
ignorance, but the extent to which they are made means that, in
that student's opinion, the variety rejected is not a form of
standard English: by definition, since standards cannot differ in
adequacy or prestige.

What then is adequacy? This refers to the degree of a speaker's
fluent control over the resources of a language—particularly the
grammatical and lexical resources. And, although adequacy

(represented as the front-back dimension of the cube) may exist in different kinds and may vary in ways that are not yet understood, we must insist that it is a dimension that is independent of the other two. That is, the three-year-old child of a standard language speaker has a command of the prestige dialect that is still seriously inadequate: he cannot string words together in the full grammatical complexity that is at his father's command, and there are thousands of words that he cannot yet use. He has not even fully mastered the phonological system. There is the inadequacy of the foreign learner, too, who may also be a speaker of the prestige dialect (insofar as he knows English at all) but who has like the native child much to learn before he can say all that the adult standard language speaker can say. And then there is the inadequate language command of the socially deprived for whom certain shades of meaning in expression are unattainable, not merely in the standard language but even in the low-prestige dialect to which his birth and upbringing have committed him.

Which brings us to this third dimension, represented as vertical on the cube model. The two dimensions so far discussed—similarity and adequacy—can in principle be described linguistically (though in all conscience we must admit that such measurement is still grossly rudimentary when it attempts to be more than intuitive). The third dimension, prestige, cannot be measured linguistically at all; and if my reading of the literature is sound, it would seem that the sociologists and socio-linguists have a long way to go before they can objectify their and our intuitions in the matter. But the dimension's existence can hardly be in question nor our intuitions. We tacitly and sometimes overtly acknowledge its relevance by not directing TESOL classes to the English of Birmingham, England—or indeed of Birmingham, Alabama. Our lexicographers acknowledge it by leaving most words unlabelled while labelling others 'dialect' or 'substandard'—and do not let us fool ourselves we can always tell the difference: dialects are often treated in effect as substandard—it is just that many substandard forms resist the geographical pigeon-holing that our usual concept of 'dialect' requires.

There may however be room for disagreement over the *independence* of the prestige dimension. Can speakers of a low prestige dialect ever attain full linguistic adequacy? Shocking as it may seem even to ask such a question, we must face the fact that in our teaching we often behave as though the answer was a resounding 'no.' The educational systems of all countries that I am familiar with strive rather singlemindedly to improve pupils' adequacy with items and patterns belonging to the standard language, and, regardless of the lip service paid to leaving the child's local language alone, measure improvement in adequacy in what amounts to solely in these terms. And our customers only too readily get the message. I have the impression that programmes for improving the English of the socially disadvantaged in this country have run into the difficulty of pupils feeling that they are not being taught greater adequacy in their own language but are being saddled with the 'white folks' talk'. But if there are practical difficulties in dissociating the prestige and adequacy dimensions, I am enough of a traditional Bloomfieldian (thanks largely to the teaching I had in this country from Bloch, Fries, Pike and Marckwardt) to believe that in an important sense the two dimensions are genuinely independent. It is in fact impossible to read the Lallans poetry of contemporary Scotland without believing them independent, or the novels of Alan Sillitoe without sharing his belief that the working class substandard speech of contemporary Nottingham is capable of the fullest sensibilities and range of expression. And you may recall that although Mellors was perfectly fluent in standard British English, he felt that only his Derbyshire dialect was adequate to loving Lady Chatterley. This point should remind us that the mastery of language for specific occasions (after the manner of Martin Joos's *Five Clocks*) is a function of the adequacy dimension, however much—as with Mellors—it operates at a fixed point of the prestige dimension.

At any rate I feel we should be in no doubt that we know pitifully little about this third dimension, prestige, and of its relation with the others; that our work in teaching English as a 'second dialect' will be dangerously vitiated unless our understanding improves; and that it is along this dimension that we must expect very significant changes during the last decades of this millennium. Not merely are we likely to witness the full status of 'standard' being conferred upon the English of Australia and other major foci of power geographically separate from the other English-speaking areas; we must see the resolution of the standardization problem in smaller areas of national identity—Hiberno-English, for example, not to mention the English of previously underprivileged groups within our national borders. Taking a world view of English is not a particularly cheering prospect nor one that can give us as linguists much ground for self-congratulation. And meantime, God help those who are at the remotest point on all three dimensions—similarity, adequacy and prestige—like the immigrant minorities in our midst.

To take only the formal description of a single variety of institutionalized standard English, the surviving problems are daunting enough, though here the linguist has more grounds to be pleased with himself—as well he might after three hundred years' continuous effort. During this three hundred years more attention has been paid to the problems associated with prescriptivism than to all the rest put together: those rather few features where we stubbornly go on using one form but teaching another, generation after generation. And even after three hundred years, we really do not know what to make of them. The traditional twentieth-century attitude was summed up in Robert Hall's title *Leave Your Language Alone*, but we do not: cannot, it seems. On the plane to Chicago this week, a professor of linguistics passed across to me a periodical, saying 'Look at this: I do not generally object to split infinitives but I draw the line well short of this one.' The quotation he had heavily ringed read *They used to annually visit the center*. The same is true of the position of *only* ('He only earned a little money' where we do *not* mean that he got most of his money more easily): 'John does not love you as much as me,' says a lad to a lass, and he does not mean that John loves *him* more. Students in TESOL classes ask us about these points but have we decided what to tell them?

Then there are the problems that are inherent in English as a living, changing and imperfect language. In speaking of a 'living' language, I am thinking of the many instances of divided usage where opinions differ as to whether one form is to be preferred to another or whether any significant difference is involved: *whether* versus *if* in dependent questions, *while* versus *whilst*, the first vowel of *either*, the spelling of *judgment* or *connection*. With my reference to 'changing' language, I have in mind transitional features like the steady growth of spelling pronunciations such as *forehead* which will no longer rhyme with little girls that are horrid; or the steady stream of words that are changing their meaning, such as *anthropoid* which has added *apelike* to its earlier meaning of *manlike*, or even grammatical changes. The great *Oxford English Dictionary* provides an unwitting example of this with the unlikely compound *knight-errant* for which it gives as the plural only the form *knights-errant*, though the neighbouring entry for *knight-errantry* (surely written by the same learned editorial hand) glosses this abstract noun as (inter alia) 'The body of knight-errants.'

And with my reference to 'imperfect' language, I have in mind not just the gaps in our phonological system, still less the imperfections in our orthography (usually exaggerated anyhow), but rather the gaps and misfits in our lexicon and grammar. Thus while we can ask a parent how many children he has without descending to the specificities of sex, we cannot ask a child how many brothers and sisters he has without requiring just this male/female distinction. If *undergarments* can have a singular *undergarment*, why cannot the far commoner plural *underclothes* be also singularized? ('When she unpacked at the Pick she was one undy short'). How do you spell 'Did they used to visit the centre'— or would you prefer to tell pupils not to write it? *These kind* of things trouble our students and anybody who *believes* otherwise *need their head* examined. Perhaps you or your friend *knows* (*know*?) the answer.

But troublesome or not, these things are peripheral. There are great and stable problems of English grammar at the core which are much more important and on which it is fair to say that our generation of linguists has made and is making considerable progress. And their solution seems to be throwing light (thanks above all to the lead given by Chomsky) far beyond the confines of English grammar to the nature of linguistic relations in general.

There are so many areas of English grammar where good work has been done in the past ten years that it is difficult to decide what to select for exemplification. But let me attempt a word on the interesting work that has recently been done, and is continuing (cf. R. Bladon, *English Studies* 49, 1968), on the non-finite verb clause: particularly the infinitival or participial form of the verb:

> He expected her to listen
> He found her listening

Here there is virtually no choice: we have to select infinitive with *expect* and participle with *find;* and this is the normal situation: most verbs require the one or the other and the temptation has been to write this off as 'idiom'—with all the mingled contempt and despair which lie behind the linguist's use of this term.

But a few verbs permit a choice: notably the polar pair *like* and *hate*

> He liked (her) $\begin{cases} \text{to listen} \\ \text{listening} \end{cases}$
>
> He hated (her) $\begin{cases} \text{to listen} \\ \text{listening} \end{cases}$

and many attempts have been made to specify the conditions under which the native speaker selects one or other form and the difference if any that is implied. Interesting demonstrations have been made of the aspectual relevance in terms of perfectivity or isolatedness on the one hand, and imperfectivity, duration, or iterativeness on the other. Thus given the two possibilities

> He heard the door $\begin{cases} \text{slam} \\ \text{slamming} \end{cases}$

and the requirement to associate with these one of the two adjuncts *all night* or *at midnight*, we would unhesitatingly associate *at midnight* with *I heard the door slam* and *all night* with *I heard the door slamming*, while admitting freely that the alternative selection would still result in acceptable sentences. But it is possible to define the selection principle still more tightly. Consider the fact that although *like* and *hate* will generally allow both infinitive and participle, there is sharp restriction as soon as conditional modality is introduced:

$$\text{I'd} \left\{ \begin{array}{l} \text{like} \\ \text{hate} \end{array} \right\} \text{her} \left\{ \begin{array}{l} \text{to listen} \\ \text{*listening} \end{array} \right.$$

This leads to the suggestion that it is not duration or iterativeness that is involved with the participle so much as *fulfilment*. (I am sorry to invoke the notions of D. H. Lawrence twice in one paper.) But it is not a simple matter of the infinitive indicating unfulfilment and the participle fulfilment: *I liked her to visit me* does not leave it in any doubt that she did in fact visit me. No: the selection involves also what the Prague School linguists called the marked and unmarked opposition. The use of the participle actually marks the action of the embedded clause as fulfilled, where the infinitive is uncommitted on the matter. This analysis satisfactorily accounts not only for our usage with verbs which present a choice—*see*, *hear*, *prefer*, *like*, *love*, *hate*—but also with the vast majority where no choice is available:

$$\text{I expected to see her} \left\{ \begin{array}{l} \text{and I did} \\ \text{but I didn't} \end{array} \right.$$

$$\text{I enjoyed seeing her} \left\{ \begin{array}{l} \text{and (of course) I did} \\ \text{*but I didn't} \end{array} \right.$$

Here, as elsewhere in applied linguistics, our problem is first to expose the system whose rules we, as fully adequate natives, control unconsciously; and second to expound this system in a way that can be understood and assimilated by our students. Not everything we know is worth teaching, but much that should be taught, we still do not 'know.' The fact that our manifold deficiencies do not depend on the work of teachers alone or linguists alone, or Americans alone, but on the collaboration of psychologists, sociologists and those with experience of English in other societies in other continents: this fact is the reason for the World View that TESOL is appropriately taking.

4 Our Changing Language

In the comfortable days of Victoria, a title like this might well have stirred people to complacent pride. A changing institution was likely to be a 'developing' one—one that was becoming bigger (and therefore better); becoming richer; in short, progressing. We have come a long way since we equated change with progress, and today we are all probably more cynical about change of any kind. So far as English is concerned, at any rate, a commoner reaction seems to be that change equals decadence. A recent correspondence in a newspaper was entitled 'The Fading Beauty and Purity of the English Language'. Still more recently, a correspondent in *The Times* felt that 'the prospect for the communication of ideas is bleak'; and another, enraged by a music leaflet about a pianist who had 'concertized in France', protested about the degradation of our linguistic heritage.

Not only, it would seem, have we ceased to draw from the well of English undefiled: excessive fluoridization of the relevant municipal supplies by responsible authorities in the redevelopment areas has given considerable rise (say official sources) to a severe overall outbreak of slattern-mouth disease, or tongue-rot.

The last thing I want to do is condone ugly writing or careless speech, or deny that there is a danger of standards falling and of an irresponsible permissiveness eroding our expression into colourless imprecision. But from time to time one does feel the need to raise a mild eyebrow at uninformed and hysterical outbursts over the alleged corruption and decadence of English today. In the first place, language is only one manifestation—however important—of human behaviour, and we deceive ourselves if we think that the cause or cure of so-called linguistic corruption lies in language alone. But of course it is equally wrong to claim that the supposed decadence of language is a symptom of everything else we deplore. 'Empty churches, won't do a decent day's work,

This paper was broadcast at the end of 1963 and published in *The Listener*, 2 January 1964.

expect the state to do everything, nothing but bingo and pools—
all of a piece with this slang and sloppiness of expression that we
get from America'. It should be obvious that such a string is not
all of a piece. If we want to blame our favourite whipping-boy
across the Atlantic for the linguistic ills we detect, we cannot
at the same time link them with other ills (empty churches,
work-shyness, for example) that do not seem to be afflicting
America.

In the second place, we need to get things a little more into
perspective by examining the extent to which our language is
changing, the ways in which it is changing, and the grounds for
thinking that change is decay. A Cabinet Minister picks his way
wearily down the steps from an aircraft. With hours of jet-whine
and pressurization still in his ears, he meets a pack of hungry
reporters. Before the day is out, the newspapers quote him to
millions as saying: 'These sort of agreements do an awful lot for
our balance of payments'. Whatever this may have sounded like
as he no doubt carefully avoided sounding pompous or unfriendly,
in merciless print the remark cannot do 'an awful lot' of good to
his reputation as a stylist, and at 'these sort of things' white
moustaches in Hove bristle over their muffins. Debasement of our
linguistic heritage again—and in high places, too. Oh for a
linguistic Denning!

Needless to say, examples of this kind offer no evidence whatever
of 'corruption' or 'debased standards', and protests reveal only
the conviction—as tenacious as it is naive—that there is a single
standard of acceptability, of 'correctness', regardless of the situation in which language is being used. The politician is berated
for his colloquial, off-the-cuff usage just as though he had written
it in a formal report published by H.M. Stationery Office. We
must remember that we all have a rich and vastly complicated
repertoire of English that varies according to whether we are with
family or strangers, with juniors or equals or seniors, whether we
are speaking or writing, what we are speaking or writing about,
etc., etc.

Some people seem to feel that there is something disreputable
about multiple standards, but they are universal in all aspects of
human behaviour, not just in language. The dinner jacket that is
'correct' for an evening reception is not correct on the cricket
field. Pretty well every man is punctilious about rising gallantly to
his feet as his wife approaches—provided he is in (let us say) a
hotel lounge. But does he do the same when she merely joins him
beside the telly? And does she think him boorish if he does not?

It is the same with language. Acceptability and correctness are
by no means irrelevant, but the standards are finely adjusted

according to a subtle social agreement about the forms that are appropriate to different occasions.

Once we have this clear, we can start thinking about this matter of change, and how much of it portends the doom of English. Talk of our corrupted, disintegrating language was current in Shakespeare's time and much of it must be written off as merely the ubiquitious 'golden-age' theme of folklore. Elders have shaken their heads over 'the young ones' since palsy began, and English is not the only language to be frowned upon. In September 1963, a writer in *The Scotsman* reported that Swedish is in a very bad way, the only hopeful point being that in Finland at least there are people who 'speak and write a far better Swedish than that found in Sweden'. It is difficult to imagine in any detail the extraordinary concept of standard in language that must lie behind pronouncements of this kind. 'My idea of a really fine symphony is *Rigoletto*'.

At the present time, anxiety about change is complicated by there being several kinds of change which are too readily conflated, and one has already been suggested: change in society and its environment. A century ago statesmen were not required to make so many pronouncements off the cuff, and there was leisure to vet them before they appeared in print. In our clock-haunted times, there is far more rapid and wholesale transfer from one medium (say, informal conversation) to another (say, a newspaper article), with less time or inclination for adjustment in terms of 'appropriateness'. We therefore *see* far more frequently forms of expression which we do not so easily notice (or so violently object to) if we hear them in conversation. Again, we have today mass media in sound or print consciously and carefully organized to address millions who were scarcely addressed at all, as it were, a century ago, and so, for this reason too, we may well read and hear more 'slang' or 'loose grammar' than was once the case. But is this popular language really more debased and corrupt than the language of the music hall to which the masses were exposed when Chevalier 'knocked 'em in the Old Kent Road'?

Then there are the changes in education. Teachers are no longer so preoccupied in sweeping the unacceptable under the desks; instead, for good or ill, they tend to encourage pupils to express themselves for ordinary purposes in the language they ordinarily use and find natural. Our children are thus less inhibited about using expressions of dubious status than their grandparents (or more particularly their great-grandparents) were; so from another angle, too, things once heard chiefly in the back-yard are heard more and more in the drawing-room, and whether they are themselves new or old, they again contribute to the impression that the language has changed.

It is commonly said that the new trends in education have resulted in a lowered standard of written English, but this is by no means as obvious as critics have alleged. Since more pupils are sitting examinations than ever before, and since the additional ones come chiefly from the least educated environments, it would not be surprising to find not merely *more* poor performances, but a *greater proportion* of poor performances. And this, even if true, would not necessarily give cause for alarm. *The Times* leader on October 17, 1963, pointed out that 'the nation's literacy, as measured by reading tests, has risen markedly since 1945'.

Moreover, many educationists claim that children are becoming proficient in areas unknown to earlier generations in primary schools. There is the wider general knowledge and the teaching of subjects like science and French which were once largely reserved for the relatively few who went on to grammar schools. Even within the subject called 'English' it is claimed that there is more realization of the child's personality and experience in his writing than there was when the neat, well-written sentences were concerned only with dull, rigid, and derivative exercises. In any case, the basis of criticism about English is often spelling, and much as we may deplore poor spelling it cannot be equated with (nor yet generally taken as an index of) poor command of language. Certainly, there are teachers who feel that plenty of compensations can be found in other aspects even of our children's performance in English.

A further change is that affecting grammarians themselves. There have come to be fewer and fewer who believe that English can be ruled from the outside, so to speak, by reference to absolute standards derived from logic, or by reference to the grammatical rules of a language (usually Latin) that was thought to have more prestige. Instead, scholars have put more and more emphasis on observing and studying English as it is actually used rather than as it 'ought' to be used; and they have especially interested themselves increasingly in spoken language. When a philologist changes his interest he does not, of course, change the language. But because the grammar-books and dictionaries that he writes ignore things previously stressed and mention things previously ignored, they can easily give the impression of change in the language itself.

To quote a single and obvious example, the 'New and Revised Edition' of Bain's *Higher English Grammar* (1875) sets out the past of 'may' as 'I might, thou mightst, he might, we might, ye might, they might'. No school grammar today would include 'thou mightst' or 'ye', but if we compare *The Return of the Native* (1878) or *The Egoist* (1877) or *Middlemarch* (1871) with some modern novels, we shall not find the language changed in these respects since the 'New and Revised Edition' of Bain appeared.

The changes discussed so far, it will be agreed, do not amount to any wholesale mutation of our language, still less to wholesale mutilation. We might well be merely illustrating Alphonse Karr's aphorism, *'Plus ça change, plus c'est la même chose'*. But, of course, in the narrow sense generally understood by 'linguistic change', English is also changing—as it always will and must while it is the daily language of a living society. No small part of a language's usefulness lies in its adaptability to its users' needs; the time to cry decadence and debasement is when the language has no more need to change.

In *The Lord of the Rings* we find that hobbits live well beyond our mortal span, and so we should not be surprised that they have developed their own special ways of numbering beyond the miserable seventy and eighty that are awesome enough for us. There were great celebrations when Bilbo Baggins became eleventy-one and Frodo thirty-three on the same day, the latter number being important because it was the coming of age, when one was expected to know how to live like a complete gentlehob-bit, having got past those awkward *tweens*. Professor Tolkien tells us that this last word was needed so that hobbits could talk about 'the irresponsible twenties between childhood and coming of age'.

What hobbits must do, we must do. New words are formed (gimmick, transistor, tele-recording), and in no time at all we are using them as familiarly as if we had known them all our lives. Old words are blithely put to new uses; Thackeray would be astonished to hear how fashionable it is to live in a mews (for him, a stable). As new fashions arise and new centres of influence develop, our language reflects the changes and we are soon 'with it', talking airily of the French fries we had with our lunchtime ham-burger. A latter-day Rip Van Winkle might be as mystified by what he heard after a year as Irving's beloved original was after twenty

And clearly the relevant 'new centre of influence' for our lang-uage is the United States. Not that this is particularly new. We have known about schooners, cockroaches, moccasins, and pumpkins for at least 200 years; we have used the words 'boss' and 'sleigh' and 'toboggan' for a good century, and we have had the dubious benefits of 'dope' for about half that period. What is new is the speed and frequency with which American expressions become acclimatized here (though 'acclimated' has not). In 1809 a cocktail was a 'recondite beverage' to Washington Irving, and it took a century for it to start becoming less recondite in England; the verb 'donate' also needed the whole of the nineteenth century to become accepted here; 'motel' took fifty years. But the disc-jockey galloped over at a fair pace and the beatnik shuffled across with a speed and urgency almost unprecedented (and certainly uncharacteristic). American expressions now rapidly become our own with ever increasing generality. What is especially significant to note is that this influence is also increasingly imperceptible. The more closely knit our systems of communication and commerce, the more words we adopt and the less aware we seem to become of doing so: and the less aware we become of differences in usage between the two areas.

It used to be thought that the chief importer of American expressions was the talking film, but it seems to me most likely that the present vast momentum of relatively imperceptible influence comes through the press. When we hear American speech in a film, after all, we are constantly reminded that it *is* American; we see the speakers in their American setting and hear their accent. But when we read 'Rocks thrown at Police' in a British headline, our defences are down: we do not notice (any more, presumably, than the sub-editor) that this comes from an American agency report, and we are the readier to adopt this use of 'rocks'. Again, as more and more of the influential members of our community trek back and forth, they unconsciously absorb American expressions and transmit them, with all the force of their authority, in their newspaper articles and broadcast talks back in Britain. 'Commuter' quietly and quickly established itself in the second half of the fifties, and one can now find 'aside from' and the verb 'contact' in the writings of men who would vigorously deny being under American influence (cf. pp. 29–30).

There is little point in protesting that there is no need for these American words—that we can get along perfectly well with 'apart from', 'get in touch with', and 'season-ticket holder'. There was no need for anyone to have fins on the back of his car a year or so ago, but it is human nature to respond to the whims of fashion. Most of our linguistic innovations, in fact, correspond to fairly important changes in our society. The word 'teenager', for instance, is a recognition that young people have come to be a social and economic force in their own right, with their own clubs, songs, dances, tastes. Of course, we had words for this 'age-group' before, but the new word focuses upon the teenagers' gaiety and vitality as distinct from their biological status (adolescent) or their penchant for delinquency (juvenile).

According to our temperament, we may like or dislike particular changes in language, just as we may like or dislike flick-up hair-do's or shift-style dresses or stainless steel table-ware, or anything else that the winds of change blow our way. But we must be clear in our minds about one thing: it is no more disreputable to be using a somewhat different daily language from that of our great-grandparents than it is to travel by Viscount instead of stage-coach.

Nor—and this may become a big issue if the Beatles really do put Merseyside accents in grace and favour—is it any more disreputable for people in different parts of the country to have corresponding differences in speech than it is for some people to live in Halifax and others in Hampstead, or for some people to be farmers and others physicians. We no longer giggle loutishly or stare with gauche, parochial disapproval at a sari or kenty cloth. The whole trend in our society has been towards a welcome acquaintance with cultural relativity—which means overcoming the impulse to thank God that we are not as other men are. It is high time that we caught up with this trend in our view of language as well, so that a realistic, tolerant perspective can replace the naive idiocies and cruel bigotries to which we are still prone.

Above all, it is this perspective that we need. It is not a question of sanctioning the undoubted sloppiness and vagueness and ugliness of expression we find around us, or the turgid pomposities in much industrial, scientific and official prose. But let us remember that, as well as the writers of pop lyrics and comic strips, we have poets and novelists with as subtle, austere, and shapely a style as ever, and that Charles Dickens had occasion to write of the Circumlocution Office as pungently as Sir Ernest Gowers.

5 Are Overseas Learners a Threat to English?

Threats to the purity and the real genius of English have been a recurrent theme for the moralists in our midst. At the close of the first Elizabethan age, Samuel Daniel's Musophilus takes up the challenge of Philocosmus, who is dismayed by the 'gawdy liu'ry' and 'nice Corruptions' in contemporary style. Musophilus argues that English should not 'come behind the rest In powre of words', foreseeing an increasingly worthy role for the language. Who, he asks,

> knowes whither we may vent
> The treasure of our tongue, to what strange shores
> This gaine of our best glory shall be sent,
> T'inrich vnknowing Nations with our stores?

He is far from unaware of the possible importance that English might come to have in remote and exotic countries (including the new world of America and the Atlantic Indies, and his rhetorical question continues with that striking absence of feeble blushing modesty that has tended to characterize Anglo-Saxon comments on the civilizing influence of English:

> What worlds in th'yet vnformed Occident
> May come refin'd with th'accents that are ours?

In the second Elizabethan age, ironically enough, it is precisely from these exotic regions that people have seen the English language most sharply threatened.

A danger often referred to—not least in the British press—is that English in vast areas such as India, Pakistan, and Africa may become seriously degenerate, an English so different from ours in the traditional English-speaking countries that we will find our language fragmenting into a number of mutually quite unintelligible dialects. The importance, after all, of attempting to use

This paper was expanded from a broadcast and subsequently published in *The Listener*, 27 September 1962.

English more and more widely in the world is to provide an international means of communication: the more pidginized the language becomes, obviously the less useful English can be as a world language.

This is a valid argument. We have all heard Indians, Pakistanis and Africans speaking English, and we all know how hard it can be to understand them and to get them to understand us.

But how valid is the allusion I have just made to 'pidginized' English in relation to the admittedly foreign-sounding English of the Indian who is studying in this country, let us say, or who is working hard to learn English in his own country? I think there is a very real distinction to be observed. But before we come on to that, let us pause here to look briefly at the *kinds* of variation that we have in a language as rich and widespread as English—variation which comprises not only Pidgin and 'broken' English but also creolized forms of the language. Take the following example:

> Hin sed den, 'Ma, a we in lib?' Him sie, 'Mi no nuo, mi pikini, bot duon luk fi hin niem hahd, or eni wie in a di wohld an yu kal di niem, hin hie unu'. Him sed, 'Wel Ma, mi want im hie mi an nuo mi'. 'Lahd nuo, masa! Duo no kal di niem, hin wi kom kil yu!' Him sie, 'Wel Ma, hin wi haf fi kil mi'.
>
> [He said then, 'And where does he live, Mother?' 'I don't know, my child,' she said, 'but don't look hard for his name, or anywhere in all the world that you call the name, he will hear you'. 'Well, Mother,' he said, 'I want him to hear me and know me.' 'Heavens, no, sir! Don't call the name: he'll come and kill you.' 'Well, Mother,' he said, 'he'll have to kill me'.]

That is one variety of the language which is recognizably English, whatever difficulties we may have in understanding it at first. Here is another specimen, to remind us that not all the extreme varieties of English originate abroad:

> Nah Juabz midlin thik layk, bur iyd a ad ta bi a diyal thika nat ta noh at tha wa sumat rang tweh at shu wa prehchin on, an soh i lat pehpa tuml ontat flua an i sat thiyr an gehpt wol shu stopt fa briyath, an then i sez, 'Wot tha hek az ta ageht on, las? Iz tha sumat up a sumat?'
>
> [Now Job is pretty stupid, but he'd have had to be a good deal stupider not to know that there was something wrong, because of how she was ranting on. So he let the paper tumble on to the floor and he sat there staring till she stopped for breath. Then he said, 'What on earth is the matter with you, girl? Is there something wrong or something?']

Both these are obviously very different from standard English, and it would not be easy to say which differs most, though the first is the Creole English spoken in far-away Jamaica, while the second is one of the forms of Yorkshire English, used by Englishmen not far away from the centre of England. But this is not our present concern: the point I want to stress is that both these varieties of English are quite distinct from Pidgin. True, the Creole and the Yorkshire dialect have their own special words and they have grammatical forms of their own and of course a distinctive pronunciation of their own; but they nevertheless have in common with each other and with standard English a remarkably broad area of grammatical and lexical material. At all the points where we seem to have difficulty in understanding the Jamaican and Yorkshire forms, we can state the grammatical forms that we would use in our own variety of English: however different the creolized or dialectal forms may be, they almost always have a one-for-one correspondence to standard English forms. All of this amounts to saying that there is close similarity of structure here.

In Pidgin, we find a very different situation. Even granting that Pidgin has many words that we recognize easily, the crucial fact is that both in grammar and vocabulary Pidgin has deeply engrained distinctive features which are quite institutionalized, as we say, and which mark it off consistently from Standard English, Creole and Yorkshire English alike; see Chapter 6.

To return now to the English that is being learnt in India and Africa: it is certainly very different from our own, but for the most part its distance from our own is much less than Jamaican Creole shows—or even Yorkshire English. And of course still less is it to be compared with Pidgin. The Indian usually speaks a form of English that is 'full' in a very obvious sense: it has a large vocabulary, identical for the most part with that of standard English; it has a grammar which differs scarcely at all from standard English; the more educated the Indian, the more likely it is that the differences lie only in pronunciation.

But not all Indians are educated and there is no denying that Pidgin exists in India and Africa as well—but the context is very different from that of Pidgin in New Guinea: Pidgin is not so widespread or dominant as to show likelihood of becoming the model, an end in itself. In the Indian and African countries, we find an even spectrum of kinds of English, which extends from those most like Pidgin to those most like standard English, with imperceptible gradations the whole way along. However halting and minimal his command of English may be, a person in these countries is to a greater or lesser degree in contact with someone else whose English is a little better. And at the top of the scale, we get a man like Mr Nehru, speaking an English perfectly comprehensible and acceptable throughout the English-speaking world.

Let us look in rather more detail at the situation in Ghana, which I visited recently. I was struck there by precisely this enormous range of English. At the top there was President Nkrumah, proclaiming English as the language of education for the entire country and himself the master of a good, full English immediately recognizable as standard. From the President, members of his cabinet and the professions, the gradations of competence in English were infinite, down ultimately to the long-shoreman, the docker, or the man who has a little café on the waterfront and whose English is learnt pidgin-wise, dealing with restricted matters in the course of elementary contact with European sailors: the man who says things like 'no be so' for 'that's not true', or 'I go-come', meaning 'I'm going but I'll be back in a moment '(as opposed to 'I go-go'—'I'm going and I'm not coming back', 'I'm going for keeps'); the man who uses 'pass-all' as the superlative sign ('good pass-all' meaning 'best') or 'bad' in the sense of 'very' ('sweet bad' meaning 'very sweet').

This kind of English is in fact called Pidgin in Ghana: people explicitly distinguish it from a fuller local variety of English that might be called Ghanaian English, the English used by ordinary people in the middle range of education. Naturally, the full Ghanaian English covers a wide range of usage itself. Some speakers admit many Pidgin words into their usage, and one common transfer from Pidgin concerns the expression 'I go-come' that I mentioned just now. Many competent speakers of English in Ghana can be heard saying 'I am coming' in this same sense—that is, 'I'm going but will be back immediately'. So although this Ghanaian English does not in the least resemble Pidgin in being a language equipped only for restricted dealings in trade and the like, nevertheless has specifically African and Ghanaian characteristics which distinguish it—as all other varieties of English are distinguished the world over.

'Quiet', for example, is used in the sense of 'peaceable', and 'too' often means 'very ', so that 'He is too quiet' means 'He is very gentle'. You may hear a man saying that he has 'convinced' someone to do something—meaning 'persuaded' him to do it. At times the visitor may be misled into thinking that an African is speaking in a joking, facetious way when he says, for instance, 'My wife has brought forth', but we find that this quaintly digni-fied expression is being used quite seriously. The steering wheel of a car is called a 'steer' and the verb to 'bluff' often does not convey what we mean by the word but rather to 'show off', to dress and walk with some spirited showiness—'He came bluffing down the street'. His pride may derive from his having spent some time abroad—studying in the United Kingdom perhaps; if so, he may be referred to with the rather derisive Ghanaian expression, 'He's a been-to'.

Prestige and status are reflected in other ways too. Our language everywhere of course uses the suffix '-ful' to form adjectives like 'beautiful', but in the colloquial speech of Ghana one finds such expressions as 'They are car-ful' or 'They are fridge-ful', indicating that a family has reached the status in society that is indicated by the possession of a car or a refrigerator. More seriously, we have the use of 'stool' as a symbol of authority, along with the compound words to 'enstool' and the noun 'enstoolment'; similarly, 'skin', 'enskin', and 'enskinment' are used with reference to the purely African situation of a chief's authority and the manner in which it is invested. Then there is—as in India —the distinctive use of the word 'bungalow'. At first glance, it would seem to be in contrast with the Ghanaian English word 'storey-building' —meaning a building which has more than one storey. But this is not so. The meaning of 'bungalow' has nothing to do with the number of floors—bungalows in Ghana may have only one floor but probably more often have two or three: it has to do rather with the *status* of the building, as the home of a senior official.

I need scarcely add that none of these expressions can be regarded as 'broken' English or anything of that kind. They are the distinctive parts of a worthy and serious whole: a self-respecting, established variety of English—different of course from British or American varieties but sharing much with them and little with Pidgin. At the same time it is a variety of English with this astonishing range that I mentioned earlier and which must constantly be born in mind. Talking on the telephone in Accra, one often becomes aware at once that there is a Ghanaian on the other end of the line, because he makes so prominent a use of the specifically Ghanaian features. But—far more significantly —it is often impossible to tell whether the man on the phone is a Ghanaian or a European, so international a form of English exists at one extremity of the linguistic range.

It is because this range exists and because there remains in the African and Indian societies a fairly clear image of a standard, international English (however few attain it) that we can calm our fears for the future of English standards in these countries. We have in this respect something very different from the linguistic situation in a Pidgin area like New Guinea. And here is another difference. 'Neo-Melanesian' as a language is so far from English that our English orthography cannot be used: a special new orthography has been devised for it which both fits the language and also serves to emphasize the sharp split from English ('Gud nius Mark i raitim'—'The Gospel according to St Mark'). There have been no serious proposals to spell English in India or Africa with a new orthography, and the mere fact that Indians and Englishmen *spell* the language alike has a considerable centripetal influence on the language in other respects too; it helps to keep English together and keep Pidgin at bay, so to speak.

In short, while we certainly find many Africans and Indians for whom Pidgin is the closest they come to English, they get no reinforcement, no endorsement of such language from the educated establishment and there is little danger that their kind of Pidgin will supersede English and become the standard. The Ghanaian who uses forms like 'I go-come' and 'No be so' may not have much personal contact with people whose English is more like ours, but at least he will not be encouraged in his kind of usage by any book that he reads, by any official document that he gets, or by any news broadcast that he hears. Any tendency to change is more likely to be in what we would think of as an upward direction from his near-Pidgin usage, through broad local Ghanaian English, perhaps even to the kind of international English that his leaders use: his newspapers, his children's teachers, his government's officials, even his radio entertainment would all tend to pull him in that direction. There is no more danger, one might argue, that the Pidgin spoken on the Accra waterfront will become the English of Ghana than there is that the speech of the Limehouse or Wapping waterfront will become the Queen's English and be used as the regular medium on the BBC. Perhaps less.

6 That's Their Pidgin

At first sight the study of Pidgin English seems very marginal within the field either of English or of language more generally. It is a form of communication used by relatively small numbers (the greatest concentration is in New Guinea where there are not much more than half a million speakers), relatively remote from the major Anglo-American centres of English usage. Yet, quite apart from reasons based on social responsibility to a community of language users the vast majority of whom are educationally and economically underprivileged, there are several grounds for regarding the study of Pidgin as highly important. It provides us with an extreme example of interaction between peoples and languages producing a grammatical and lexical structure of extraordinary interest, not least to students of English linguistic history who may in consequence better appreciate the convulsive impact of French on English in the post-Conquest period. And it provides us with unique material for a sociolinguistic case study of the point at which society is concerned about recognizing the identity and dignity of a newly emerged language (as distinct from a minor uneducated dialect on the one hand or irregular, inaccurate attempts at someone else's language on the other).

But let us begin by clearing away some common misconceptions about the nature and origin of Pidgin. First, the nature. Pidgin has three notable characteristics: (1) it has a similarity to English while being obviously different; (2) one of the differences is that it seems to have some of the structure and vocabulary of languages other than English; (3) another of the differences is that it seems to be simpler than our ordinary English. But it is possible for a form of language to have any or all of these characteristics without its being thought Pidgin. British and American English manifest the first in relation to each other without Englishmen or Americans thinking that the others are speaking Pidgin. A Dane does not think that a Swede is speaking Pidgin Danish. A Manxman who says 'Goy, it's yourself that's in, yessir!' ('Heavens, so it's you, old fellow!') is obviously showing the first characteristic, and less obviously the second, with the use of an underlying Celtic structure; but again no one says he is speaking Pidgin. All three characteristics are involved when most of us speak a foreign language:

> 'Combien oranges?'

(simplified structure pronounced with a good deal of English phonology) to which we may get the reply:

> 'One franc the piece'

(with some French phonology and French idiom).

There are well-known social, political and linguistic reasons for not associating these examples with Pidgin. The British and American varieties of English are reciprocally recognized as *standards*; the Manxman is said to be speaking a *dialect* of English; Danish and Swedish are called different *languages*; the British tourist and the French shopkeeper are said to be speaking *poor French* and *poor English* respectively. But undoubtedly this last example seems to be getting closer to the idea of Pidgin. Let us take a further example which may help to pinpoint the similarity and the all-important difference.

If we have an Italian au pair girl living with us, we do not react to her imperfect English by responding to her fragmentary remarks with equally fragmented imperfect English. We speak to her rather slowly, of course, and more distinctly than we would to our family: often more simply. But we do not use with her an English that we would regard as deviant. We expect her English to improve by our example and gradually it does.

Unless we have some experience of foreign language teaching, however, most of us are in some danger of thinking that the person who speaks our language imperfectly is a little quaint or inferior and sometimes not a little stupid. Or deaf: and we may be tempted to raise our voices. When we are dealing with foreigners of radically different race or culture—and especially when we may observe some superficial aspect of material way of life that seems inferior to our own—the danger of adopting a patronizing lordliness is acute and virtually universal. And the humbler our own education, the more confident our lordly assumptions. It is against this background of human imperfection that we can best understand how there emerged Pidgin versions of Portuguese or English or Dutch.

It is not difficult to reconstruct the situation when post-medieval navigation took European ships into remote oriental ports. Uneducated crews, imbued with European prejudices and preconceptions, had to communicate with peoples looking, sounding and behaving in ways that were totally unfamiliar and—as would all too readily be presumed—grossly inferior. The Europeans would be as unlikely to condescend to learn the language of these quaint-seeming people as they would be to think them intelligent enough to learn the European language. And doubtless the local inhabitants endorsed and reinforced this humiliating valuation of themselves, honouring their Western visitors as superior, whether or not sincerely, whether or not through natural courtesy or a desperate desire to trade. At any rate they showed themselves willing to learn enough of whichever language the sailors were using; enough for basic commercial purposes; and enough—as this theory has it—to convince the sailors that they were indeed dealing with an inferior breed of men.

For while their first steps in (say) English were neither more nor less halting than a modern au pair girl's, their hearers and in effect teachers—the ignorant but conceited sailors—were less enlightened than we are with our au pair girl. In the first place the learners were confronted with a largely substandard model of English full of sailors' slang and coarseness.

'This feller belongs to me', says a sailor, pointing to a fish. 'I gorrim at high warer'.

'Dis pela work belong him', says a local, learning fast. 'Him laze baga'. By which he hopes to convey 'That is *his* job—he is a lazy man', with no more thought of linguistic indecorum than John O'Grady's fictitious Australian immigrant from Italy who took some time to realize that the name of Sydney's Soho was not in fact King's Bloody Cross.

In the second place, when they came out with such imperfect first attempts at imitating their visitors, the sailors readily assumed that this was as good an attempt as they would ever achieve and returned the imitation compliment by mimicking the imperfect phrase. Not unnaturally, this in turn reinforced the imperfection by seeming to assure the locals that they had learned the sailor's language. 'If the masterful foreigner is speaking that way too, I must have got it right.' Pidgin English has come into being.

Anyone who doubts the plausibility of this account of things need only consider the mid-nineteenth century representation of a kindly and well-disposed Londoner addressing herself to a European's language-learning difficulties; he may then reflect whether, kindly or not, our countrymen would treat Asian or African learners more intelligently or sympathetically. The attitude of Bleeding Heart Yard to the Italian, John Baptist Cavaletto ('scantily acquainted with the most necessary words of the only language in which he could communicate' with these people) is comic but hardly unrepresentative. Ordinary Londoners 'had a notion that it was a sort of Divine visitation upon a foreigner that he was not an Englishman, and that all kinds of calamities happened to his country because it did things that England did not, and did not do things that England did' (*Little Dorrit*, Ch. 25). But, heroically repressing such convictions, the folk of Bleeding Heart Yard 'began to accommodate themselves to his level . . . treating him like a baby, and laughing immoderately at his lively gestures and his childish English . . . They spoke to him in very loud voices as if he were stone deaf. They constructed sentences, by way of teaching him the language in its purity, such as were addressed' (here Dickens misses the implication of his own insights) 'by the savages to Captain Cook, or by Friday to Robinson Crusoe. Mrs Plornish was particularly ingenious in this art; and attained so much celebrity for saying "Me ope you leg well soon", that it was considered in the Yard, but a very short remove indeed from speaking Italian.'

A further anecdotal piece of evidence in the same direction is given in a contemporary source (Laycock 1970) where we find an Australian soldier's attempt at a narrative in pidgins. In the space of a dozen lines he uses *heap* as an intensifier three times (as in 'heap silly') though this does not occur in Pidgin and, as Laycock suggests, the soldier presumably wished this on Pidgin from his second-hand knowledge of supposedly typical Red Indian speech in American cowboy fiction. The underlying idea is that what one indigenous people might do in broken English, another must surely do.

Now of course there may just be something in this. It is possible that common features in widely dispersed pidgins result from a natural filtering process, analysing by consensus and so yielding a 'basic' English lexical and grammatical structure. This would plausibly account for the general derivation from *he has* (*not*) *got* of a kernel item which is used as the verb of possession (*mi gat kanu* 'I own a canoe'), as the existential formula (*i-gat wanpela Got tasol* 'there is only one God', *no gat man i-stap* 'there is no one here'), and as the nominal or adverbial negative particle (*nogat* 'nothing', *nogat tru* 'not true'). Indeed, some theorists claim that it is the similarity in circumstance and in mental development of most Pidgin speakers that conditions the similarity in linguistic form as well as more general characteristics such as tendencies towards 'simplicity' and 'concreteness' (see Wurm 1972). The hypothesis in the present discussion, however, prefers to explain the internal characteristics of a particular Pidgin by reference to social and linguistic factors and it would consider the mobility of the 'teacher' as being of central importance in attempting to explain the general world-wide similarities between pidgins. That is, when a European trader in Hong Kong has found that he can make himself understood in this kind of English (and takes some pride in his linguistic prowess for having learnt it), what is to stop him assuming that he possesses the key to communicate with other exotic foreigners—with the inhabitants of any tropical or oriental port? When he gets to Bangkok or Rabaul or Lagos, he forcefully and confidently shouts his needs in Pidgin: it works, the locals learn it, Pidgin is spread, and the European is consolidated in his belief that he was right to spread it. This accounts for the rather close similarity in vocabulary, grammar and even phonology between the pidgins used in ports thousands of miles apart:

> Me no like look-look thatsal

would mean 'But I don't want to stare' equally in West Africa and Melanesia, with *me* as first person singular pronoun for both subject and object; *no* used for negation; reduplication (*look* plus *look*) as an intensifier device; the English tag *that's all* ('tasol') used as an adversative or concessive conjunct. Nor is it only English elements in Pidgin that show this geographical range: the ultimately Portuguese items *savvy* and *pikinini* are well-known examples of 'world Pidgin'. More pervasively, the pidgins seem universally to bear the social marks of their origin: a lexicon preoccupied with the menial, frequently brutal, innocently coarse, and in scores of ways reflecting the bullying role of the original teachers. For example the sentence *Klos i-drai hariap*, which means 'The clothes are drying rapidly', suggests the way in which the meaning of the adverb *hariap* has been deduced from European imperatives involving 'Hurry up!'

At the same time we need not be surprised that in some respects a Pidgin may be much more local, bearing especially the impress of the local language that is its users' mother tongue: *dash* 'a gift' occurs widely in West African pidgins but not in Melanesia; *oyibo* 'a white man' is common in Nigerian Pidgin but is not general in West Africa; *guria* 'an earthquake' occurs in Melanesian Pidgin but scarcely elsewhere.

It will doubtless have been noticed that examples used so far have sometimes resembled English in spelling while others have not. Rather unsettled habits of spelling are a characteristic of Pidgin and although this fact is relatively trivial in comparison with data on the vocabulary or grammar, it has its wider significance in relation to the general status of Pidgin and it is a point to which we shall return.

For the present however it may be useful to look a little more closely at some of the more important grammatical and lexical features of Pidgin. We shall concentrate on the forms widely used in Papua and New Guinea rather than in West Africa or elsewhere, partly because Melanesian Pidgin has been more fully and systematically described in print than other pidgins (cf. Hall 1943 and 1955, Mihalic 1957) and partly because the social and political implications have been brought so sharply into public discussion over the past twenty years.

Considering that the word order in Pidgin is virtually the same as in English and that the elements which are used to show grammatical relations are virtually all derived from English, it is extraordinary how sharply dissimilar the grammar of Pidgin is. In place of the formidable set of auxiliary verb usages (for tense, aspect, voice, mood), Pidgin has a number of particles derived from adverbial expressions such as 'by and by' (*baimbai* or *bai*), 'altogether' (*olgera*), from lexical verbs such as 'stop' (in the sense of 'stay'), and 'finish', or from clauses such as 'it is good'. Since Pidgin verbs do not inflect, the status of such 'auxiliary' items can be disputed, but in that they are positionally more variable and etymologically more heterogeneous than what seem more reasonably the verbs of Pidgin, it is probably sounder to regard them as adverbial particles. For example:

(a) bai(mbai) yumi go   'We shall go'
(b) mi stap rit   ⎫   'I am reading' (semantically,
(c) mi rit i-stap   ⎭   *read* + *stay*)
(d) i-gut mi wok   'I'd better work, I must work'
(e) ol i-wok pinis   'they have worked' (i.e. *work* + *finish*)
(f) mi no inap wok   'I can't work' (i.e. *enough* + *work*)

But some English auxiliary usages are paralleled closely in Pidgin:

(g) mi no ken wok   'I can't work'
(h) larim em i-kam   'let him come'

and *bin* (English 'been') is sometimes used as a past tense auxiliary:

(i) mi bin baiim kaikai 'I bought food'

One outstanding item used in the manner of an auxiliary verb, *save*, is not from English:

(j) mi no save mekim   'I can't fix the engine'
     ensin i-gut gen

No attempt is being made here to give a brief sketch of Pidgin grammar in all respects, but two further notable features are in fact illustrated in the examples (a)–(j). Since much of Pidgin grammar strikes one as a simplification of English, these two are especially worth mentioning, evincing as they do a greater complexity than English has.

One of these is the verb system which although generally simpler than in English has two affixes unknown in English. There is the 'predication prefix' *i-* which is used in all clauses with a third person subject, as in (e). Since there is no verb *to be* in present tense use, predication in a sentence meaning 'The man is hungry' is expressed solely by this prefix:

> Man i-hangre

and this explains its occurrence in (j) the latter part of which has the structure 'make the engine [be] good again'. And there is the 'transitive suffix' *-im* which as in (i) and (j) follows any verb that is being used transitively or causatively.

The second grammatical feature to be mentioned is the pronoun system. Although simpler than English in having no subject–object distinction (*mi* corresponds to both 'I 'and 'me'), it is more complex in having a contrast between inclusive and exclusive pronouns. For example, *yumi*, as in (a), includes the person(s) addressed, as distinct from *mipela* which excludes the listener(s), though both of course would be translated by *we* in English.

To turn now to the vocabulary, it is important to realize that, beneath the disguise, the vast majority of Pidgin words are of English origin. The disguise may be phonological (for example, English *f-* is replaced by a sound nearer to *p-*: *pela* for *fellow*), or semantic (for example, *poman*, from *foreman*, usually means 'partner, mate'), or grammatical (as when in (e) *pinis* from *finish* is used as an aspectual marker or when an originally phrasal verb 'cover him up' is given its Pidgin transitive suffix to yield *kara-mapim* 'to conceal'). Compounding is fairly common, as in *biksolwara* 'ocean', from *big*, *salt*, and *water*, or *toknogutim* 'to insult', or *luksave* 'to recognize' and compounds deriving from phrasal verbs are especially characteristic: for example, *bagarapim* 'to ruin' (from *bugger up*), *eramautim* 'to divulge' (from *air him out*), *kirapim* 'to rouse' (*get up*). The large number of originally phrasal verbs incorporated in Pidgin is an index of its roots in colloquial speech, especially the uninhibited idiom of working men. This is reflected in other types of compound also, such as *sithaus* 'latrine'.

Numerous compounds involve reduplication as in *lukluk* 'gaze', *puspus* 'to copulate', *tantanim* 'to spin' (i.e. to turn something round and round). Insofar as this is not a universal feature in language (there seems no mutual influence with West Africa's *go go* 'to go permanently' as distinct from *go come* 'to go tempo-rarily', for example), it may be the result of influence from indi-genous languages which have in any case provided Pidgin with a good many examples: *limlimbur* 'to stroll', *kaikai* 'food', for instance. Local oriental languages provide in fact about one sixth of the Pidgin vocabulary, a poor second to English from which three quarters of the word stock is derived but comfortably ahead of German which provides less than one twentieth. Traces of the Kaiser's rule ('long Jermantaim' legally terminated with the mandate to Australia in 1920) survive in *Kaiser* itself, *raus(im)* 'to get out', *blaistik* 'pencil', *surik(im)* 'to move back' (from *zurück*), *popai* 'to slip, overshoot' (from *vorbei*). In most cases, however, such words are being replaced rather rapidly by English words which seem to be adopted on an ever increasing scale, particularly of course via Australia.

It has already been pointed out that much of this English vocabulary suggests blunt and coarse models together with bully-ing and extreme social disparity in the earliest contacts with English speakers: the fact that the verb 'to be silent' is *sarap* (from *shut up*) can be added to the many pieces of evidence presented in examples so far. More recent adoptions from English have happily suggested contacts on a more civilized level: *skul* 'school, lesson', *kalenda*, *kontrak*, *faunten pen*, *tekewe* 'subtraction' (*take away*), *conpesio* 'confession', and *sekbuk* 'cheque-book', to round off the list with a reminder that the civilization excludes neither God nor mammon. The layers of vocabulary and the composition of the layers are as informative in studying the sociology of the Pidgin speakers as the corresponding data on 'loan words' in Middle English are in relation to language and society in medieval England. And just as in the linguistic history of England we see vacillation between adopting a ready made word and analysing the new notion into its component parts, so too in Pidgin beside examples like *conpesio* we have analytic strings such as *masin bilong mekim lektrik* instead of 'dynamo', *paitim long masin* instead of 'to type' (semantically 'strike on the machine', since *pait* has a more generalized meaning than its original, *fight*), or *klinpasin* ('cleanfashion' instead of 'chastity').

It is usual to explain the word 'Pidgin' as being itself a pidgin-ized mutant of the word *business* and although this etymology is disputable its plausibility lies to no small extent in the fact that Pidgin certainly seems to have emerged for the purposes of trade. But the more recent developments in its vocabulary, of which we have just seen some examples, indicate the present use of the language at the threshold of education, technology, administra-tion, and general advancement. Religion is taught by means of

Pidgin and Bible translations have been published. For example, from *Gud Nius Mark i Raitim* (St Mark's Gospel, Ch. 5, 30 ff):

Na Jesus i save stret,	And Jesus knew straightaway,
samfela strong bilong Em	something strong of his
i lusim Em,	had left him,
na kwiktaim Em i raun	and quickly he turned round
long ol i banisim Em,	to all who hemmed him in,
i spik: Husat i holim mi?	he said: Who is it touched me?
Na boi bilong Em ol i tok:	And his men all said:
Yu lukim bigfela lain	you see the huge crowd ('line')
ol i fasim yu,	all pinning you,
na olsem wonem yu tok:	and all the same what you say is:
Husat i holim mi?	Who is it touched me?
Na Jesus Em i lukluk raun	And Jesus gazed round
i lukim meri	to see the woman
i mekim disfela.	who had done this.

Beside that piece of very simple narrative, it may be interesting to compare the mustard-seed parable (St Mark Ch. 4, 31 f) which is less easy to match with a word-for-word translation:

Taim disfela pikanini	When this baby [seed]
i foldaun long graun,	falls into the ground,
em i liklik mo,	it is very small ('more little'),
i no get nadafela	there is no other one
i liklik olsem.	that is so small.
Tasol i go long graun,	But it is sown,
i gerap,	it grows ('gets up'),
na i kamap bigfela	it becomes ('comes up') big
winim olgeda adafela diwai,	beats entirely other plants ('trees'),
na han bilong em i bigfela,	and its branches ('hands') are big,
inap olgeda	quite enough so that
pisin bilong skai	the birds ('pigeons') of the sky
i ken wokim	can make ('work')
bet hait	a hiding place ('bed hide')
long em.	because of it.

The language of grim prophecy (Ch. 13, 14) is still less susceptible to literal rendering:

Na long taim yufela lukim	And at the time [when] you see
fasim nogud	the evil behaviour ('fashion nogood')
bilong bakarapim samting	of destroying everything ('bugger up something')

i kamap long ples	it will occur where
em i no bilong i stap long em	it has no business to be ('stop')
(Ol i kauntim disfela i mas save gud),	(All who read ('count') this must thoroughly understand it),
ol i stap long Judea	all who are in Judea
ol i mas ranawe	they must all run away
i go long maunten.	towards ('to go to') the mountain.

It may be of interest to compare this last example with its original (in the Douay Bible):

> And when you shall see the abomination of desolation, standing where it ought not: he that readeth let him understand: then let them that are in Judea, flee unto the mountains.

But of course religious matter is only a small part of the material printed and published in Pidgin during recent years. There are manuals of carpentry, mechanics, music and medicine. Pidgin is the general key to literacy in the Territory: there is some translation of standard European literary materials and even a little indigenous literature. And it is the language also of 'numeracy'; thus the sum $6 + 5 = 11$ can be taught as:

> Bungim sikis wantaim faiv (or Skruim sikis long faiv), wanem namba baimbai i-kamap? Wanpela wan.

and $40 \div 5 = 8$ as:

> Brukim (or Katim) fopela ten long faiv, haumas baimbai i-stap? Et.

But printed Pidgin is most pervasively transmitted by the press, with such newspapers as *Nu Gini Tok Tok*. A typical eight-page issue of 10 September 1969 reflects on its front page the involvement of the people in the complex interracial problems with all the trappings, technical, administrative, and of course linguistic, of present-day government:

FOA PELA MEMBA

IGO LONG RABAUL

Foapela Haus op Asembli Memba bilong Gazelle Peninsula i-bin lusim [*have left*] Pot Mosbi long wanpela liklik balus [*aircraft*] i-go long Rabaul long Trinde [*Wednesday* 'third day'] moning bilong dispela trabel kamap long hap [*region*] bilong ol . . .

FOA PELA MEMBA IGO LONG RABAUL

Foapela Haus op Asembli Memba bilong Gazelle Peninsula i-bin lusim Pot Mosbi long wanpela liklik balus i-go long Rabaul long Trinde moning bilong dispela trabel kamap long hap bilong ol.

Ol dispela lain mekim mekim arapela woka- Bikos long dispela dispela wokabaut long baut bilong em i-go aut kain pasin Gavman i-askim bilong Gavman olsem 45 minit pinis salim moa polis i-go

On the next page, along with more socio-political news involving the 'malti-resiol kaunsil', there is an advertisement for Trans-Australia Airlines:

Olgeta het man ['*top people*'] flai long T.A.A. Long wanem [*because*] em i namba wan balus [*aircraft*] tru [*certainly*]. Sapos yu laik flai long balus bilong TAA, yu iken kisim [*get*, 'catch'] tiket long Ofis bilong TAA long olgeta hap bilong dispela Teritori.

Olgeta het man flai long TAA. Long wanem em i namba wan balus tru. Yu mas flai long TAA tu.

Sapos yu laik flai long balus bilong TAA, yu iken kisim tiket long Ofis bilong TAA long olgeta hap bilong dispela Teritori.

Flai TAA olsem Pasin bilong Pren

319 1573/69

Advertisements for Japanese vehicles, 'Arnott's namba wan Biskit', and Rinso ('mekim samting bilong yuw ait tru na klin tru'), let alone strip cartoons ('Mickey Mouse na pren bilong em: long Walt Disney'), remove any further doubts we may have about Pidgin as an efficient medium of Western civilization.

It may seem both trivial and digressive to raise at this point the question, 'Is Pidgin English?', but I hope to show that this question is highly relevant to the present study and raises very serious issues indeed. That the answer is not wholly obvious may appear from the way in which we normally speak of 'Pidgin English' while it has probably not seemed absurd that in the discussion up to this point we have discussed Pidgin as though it were an entirely different language, in need of translation, with its own lexicon and grammar. And its own spelling. Perhaps this last more than anything else makes it easier for us, glancing back over the Pidgin examples, to regard it as a separate language, less obviously a 'dialect' of English. In much the same way, when we are reading samples from our linguistic history, we are more inclined to acknowledge Shakespearian language and even Chaucerian language as English than the language of Ælfric or Alfred, couched as it is in a radically different spelling system. 'Old English' as a label for this we may be prepared to take on trust, but 'Anglo-Saxon' seems to many people more natural for a language so obviously, visually different.

The point at which variant forms of a single language become different languages is not of course determined by spelling, but, given the prestige that literacy has long had in Western civilization, spelling is an important public criterion of linguistic independence and self-respect. We need only recall the long and turbulent debate in post-Renaissance West Europe—not least in England— over standardizing the vernaculars and hence justifying their serious and learned use. Now already it will have been noticed that the New Guinea Pidgin examples do not present as regularly ossified a spelling system as modern French or English do. We have had *pela* as well as *fela*; *olgera*, *olgeda*, *olgeta*; the predication prefix sometimes hyphenated, sometimes a separate word, and sometimes joined to the verb as in *iken*. But at least such forms have had a consistently sharp difference from the English 'parent' forms, and a moment's thought will help us realize that far more is involved here than a spelling that is closer to local pronunciation. If we were to write in English orthography

Ol dispela masin i-no gutpela 'These machines are defective'

it would be difficult to decide just how to do it:

All this fellow machine he no good fellow
All these fellow(s) machines they no good fellows

and any such version could only seem comically barbarous. French people would have the same problem if they had to write *J'ai une plume* with only classical Latin orthography and grammar (*Ego habeo unam plumam*) as a model. The *i* in *i-no gutpela* can not be equated to English *he*, except historically. For Pidgin itself the connexion is as irrelevant as it is for modern English that the *-s* of *backwards* and the *-ce* of *once* were at one time identical with the genitive inflexion as in *John's hat*. The largely regular and phonemic spelling in which Pidgin is written is thus a recognition that it is *not* merely a grossly imperfect form of English but a language so different that its own grammatical, lexical and orthographic conventions must be learnt if it is to be comprehensible.

There could be only one alternative: for the Papuans to be taught English in place of Pidgin and for educational development then to proceed in English, with direct access to the wealth of suitable materials already available in that language. This is an alternative that can commend itself to people who already speak English well and to whom the difficulties likely to be encountered by the Papuans (already with a general mastery of Pidgin in addition to having a local mother tongue) are not easily or readily appreciated: but would the inhabitants of France find it practicable to replace French by Latin?

The alternative commends itself also, however, for rather more sophisticated reasons to idealists the world over who wish to see 'underdeveloped' peoples having the fullest opportunities for social progress as seen in terms of conventional twentieth-century civilization. To them the world-language status of English makes it seem an incomparably better bargain for Papua and New Guinea, and other Pidgin or Creole speaking territories, than the perpetuation of an originally 'disreputable' and 'debased' patois. On this view, any move to stabilize, recognize, institutionalize Pidgin would be gross neo-colonialism, aimed at keeping underdeveloped societies in an inferior and dependent capacity. It is a respectable argument, drawing attention to real dangers, and we need not be surprised that it seemed strong enough to justify a United Nations resolution in 1953 that Pidgin be 'abolished'.

The Australian government, viewing its responsibilities pragmatically while seeing the force of these diametrically opposed viewpoints, has evolved a sensible and sophisticated compromise. On the one hand, it has devoted very considerable resources to ensuring that English can be used effectively as the medium of instruction throughout virtually the whole education system, including of course the newly-established University of Papua and New Guinea, near Port Moresby. But at the same time the Australians have recognized that only through Pidgin can the ordinary people be given speedy access to basic skills and be induced to participate in modern economic development. Well aware of the danger that too exclusive a reliance on participation through English can lead in former imperial territories to the emergence or perpetuation of a powerful élite, sharply marked off from the uneducated masses, they have encouraged the publication of news and popular materials in Pidgin and taken similar steps to give its users confidence and self-respect. In this, of course, they are continuing the policy of the leading missionary organizations (cf. Turner 1972, Ch. 10).

Now if Pidgin was to have any respectable currency for workaday and social purposes, it was important that it should shed the inappropriate chrysalis that sought to constrain it as a misshapen English. It had to be given a projection which, if not encouraging its speakers to be actually proud of their language, at least removed any grounds they might have for feeling ashamed of it. There can be little doubt that the new orthography aids the literacy campaign: that indeed fluent literacy for Pidgin speakers is difficult to imagine without it. It seems likely that the independent 'Gestalt' of the orthography encourages local self-respect and—in its recognition of Pidgin grammatical and lexical use—makes it easier for the expatriate English-speaker to avoid the temptation of thinking that Pidgin is just a crude and simplified English. In pointing so clearly the differences between Pidgin and English, all the steps that have been taken to institutionalize Pidgin may well, ironically, help Pidgin speakers to master English the world language more rapidly and efficiently. The serious attention given by expatriates to Pidgin is not just a sop to local feeling: it is a recognition of hard linguistic facts.

It is against this background that we can understand one of the answers given to the question 'Is Pidgin English?'. R. A. Hall's answer was 'No, it is Neo-Melanesian'. Whether this additional attempt to provide status and respect by onomastic fiat was as fitting as the somewhat analogous emergence of the language names 'Afrikaans' or 'Nynorsk', time alone can show. It has however undoubted congruity with the other changes that have taken Pidgin from harbour and market to the door of the 'bikskul' and the 'malti-resiol kaunsil'.

REFERENCES

R. A. Hall, Jr. *Melanesian Pidgin English* (Baltimore, 1943).
R. A. Hall, Jr. *Hands Off Pidgin English* (Sydney, 1955).

D. Laycock, 'Pidgin English in New Guinea', in *English Transported*, ed. W. S. Ramson (Canberra, 1970).

F. Mihalic, *Grammar and Dictionary of Neo-Melanesian* (Techny, Ill., 1957).

G. W. Turner, *The English Language in Australia and New Zealand*, 2nd ed. (London, 1972).

S. Wurm, 'The Papuan Linguistic Situation', in *Current Trends in Linguistics* 8 (The Hague, 1972).

7 English in Twenty Years

The Institute of Linguists has posed a wholly valid question in seeking to look ahead towards English in twenty years, and though I would have preferred to stand around the tent rather than be cast in the role of crystalgazer myself, I find the exercise of enforced speculation by no means uncongenial. But let us be clear from the outset that it is indeed speculation that is involved—and speculation in a field where a linguist's guesses may be better than someone else's only because he is likely to realize how little depends on purely linguistic factors. I shall return to this point in a moment.

In addition to being purely speculative, the title I am given is also ambiguous:

(a) How different will English be in 20 years; and
(b) How different will the role of English be in 20 years.

We have here not merely two questions, but two questions that are in principle utterly independent of each other. It would not require a very high-level conference in Europe to discontinue the practice of using the word 'copyright' on the verso of title pages, replacing it with *Verlagsrecht* or *Droits réservés*, but this diminution of the role of English in Stuttgart or Paris could not be expected to trigger off a change in the English language, even a change correspondingly minuscule. Nor could the decision to discontinue the teaching of English in *lycées* and *Gymnasien* make English sound different in London and New York. Thus it would be perfectly possible for the language to enter a conservative period and change very little in the next generation while its role underwent radical alteration, whether contracting and diminishing or dramatically increasing and diversifying. Equally, it would be possible for the language to be convulsed by change while its role remained virtually constant. Such extremes however are very

This paper was given at the Conference entitled 'English—a European Language' organized by the Institute of Linguists in Luxembourg on 11th and 12th April 1970.

improbable. Neither the language nor its role seems to me likely to remain unchanged or undergo violent alteration. Nor does it seem to me likely that the two questions should turn out to have in practice the independence they have in principle. It is possible that (b) will depend on (a). That is to say, it is conceivable that if English changes too rapidly or in ways that our neighbours consider undesirable, governments and other organizations may become less inclined to use it for conferences or to place it before other languages in education programmes. It is even conceivable that an international organization might seek to insist on certain reforms and regularizations being carried out on English (cf. Tauli 1968) as a condition of its role being extended or maintained.

But the possibility of (b) depending on (a) is small compared with the possibility of (a) depending on (b). English could not have replaced Latin in England as the language of science and learning without in the process being adapted—by vocabulary extension, for example—to suit its extended role. It is scarcely conceivable that the role of English could undergo changes during the next 20 years without there being matching changes in the language. We should therefore speculate about changes in the role of English before turning to English itself.

But the role is in turn secondary to political and sociological decisions. This is what I meant in my first paragraph by emphasizing the relative remoteness of purely linguistic factors. I must base my speculation about role upon assumptions outside linguistics, and my assumptions are these: that Britain will become more and more closely involved with continental Europe, economically, intellectually and politically; and that English will retain in the next 20 years the degree of prestige it has enjoyed in continental Europe in the past 20 years. Whether this prestige rests upon the achievements of Carnaby Street or Cape Kennedy, on the fame of jump-jets or junkies, on Canadian nickel or Australian fruit, on happenings at MIT or LSE, is beside the point. On these assumptions I would confidently predict that English will retain its prominent place in Europe, though without these assumptions, I should not be nearly as confident. One could in fact go further and predict that English will actually increase its currency, above all for the purposes of trade, but also in scientific communication and in the everyday matters of popular culture—for example, through Eurovision. And all this even in the European countries whose mother tongue is so important a language as German or French. Already *Le Monde* produces a weekly edition in English, and much of German industry regards English as the main language of export promotion; with Britain's increasing involvement in Europe between now and 1990, English can scarcely be expected to become less relevant in France and Germany.

In the rather smaller language communities of Europe, of course, the place of English is likely to affect the daily lives of the people still more closely, with their greater dependence on contact beyond national frontiers. Already the medium for more than half the world's scientific writing and popular entertainment by radio, TV and film alike, English has a momentum which only a cultural cataclasm plus an abyss of much more than 20 years in width could seriously hamper. Given something more like a cultural boost, we may expect present uses of English to expand so that by 1990 everyone in Europe may be using, or be exposed to, English for some part of every day.

We may now turn from the subordinate to the principal question and try to estimate how the English language itself will change during this period. Here again I would like to divide the problem: in the first place, what linguistic changes are likely to follow from modifications in the European role of English; in the second place, what linguistic changes may one expect independently. In tackling the first of these, let me digress to say a little about attitudes to language learning in Britain. Estimates of an increased European role for English must naturally make Europeans reflect ruefully that the future is going to confirm Anglo-Saxons in their belief that they never need to learn a foreign language because the foreigners will obligingly learn English. I am no social psychologist nor someone inclined or qualified to speak for the *Geist* of the Island Race, but I believe profoundly that this diagnosis is wrong. Whether it is the loss of empire, or the bite at last of a century's compulsory education, or the adjustment of minds towards EEC, or package tours from Brest to Bari, British people have come not only to tolerate foreign languages but even to envy those who can speak them. The BBC increasingly broadcasts speeches by European leaders and—especially in the case of French—markedly subordinates the simultaneous or sequential translation as though to imply that this is a service for only the unfortunate few who cannot understand the original. A highlight of this development occurred during the New Year 1970 reviews of the recent past: liberal excerpts from speeches by two eminent Frenchmen, General de Gaulle and President Pompidou, were broadcast without translation at all.

It seems clear therefore that the developing role of English in Europe will have its reflexive complement in English itself: as Britain and the English language go into Europe, Europe and European languages will most assuredly travel in the opposite direction, and as more Britons know more European languages they will introduce words and phrases from these languages into English. Our language has always been receptive to such influence. It is not just that the relatively recent days of Empire gave us *bungalow*, *brahmin* and *bint*. In the Middle Ages we introduced Gallicisms in the belief that 'Jack would be a gentleman if he knew French'. In Shakespeare's time it was again those aping the *élite* who powdered their talk with fashionable Italianate expressions. In the remainder of the twentieth century Jack will be affecting German and French not to be a gentleman, as the old proverb went, but to keep up with the Jones's. No *avant-garde* village can show off its *boutiques* and *joie de vivre* without *son et lumière*. Where anxious purists in France have been deploring 'franglais' in recent years, we shall perhaps hear retired colonels in Britain complain of the 'Frenglish' or 'Engleutsch' which is drowning the native wood-notes wild. Nor will such adoptions of German, French, Italian, Dutch and Scandinavian words be by any means random—as many of our medieval or Restoration adoptions give the impression of being. They will rather proceed from the roles English will be playing in Europe. To give a single example, if English became increasingly used for discourse on land reclamation, it would almost inevitably improve its ability to do so by adopting many of the Dutch technical terms developed over the many years of Holland's involvement in such work.

So far as linguistic changes related to the language's European role are concerned, therefore, I foresee a marked Europeanization of English, with large-scale borrowing of vocabulary, and this process will be small or widespread, gradual or rapid, according to the speed and degree of commitment with which Britain makes her progress into Europe. And I see these linguistic changes as natural corollaries of the economic and political ones: attempts at planned, controlled linguistic changes are likely to remain unwelcome to the English-speaking layman, and equally to the linguist—unless perhaps Denmark produces another Jespersen.

I come now to the changes that may befall English irrespective of Europe. And let me say at once that if my assumptions about Britain's European role are correct, I believe this last category of changes I have to discuss will be relatively small. For a number of reasons. In the first place, twenty years—as I have already indicated—is a very short period in terms of linguistic change. Secondly, no other social, political or economic factors of the magnitude of EEC seem even remotely probable. Thirdly, the most noticeable of the 'natural' linguistic changes are also the most superficial and least permanent: new slang will swagger in and out as boldly as ever, attracting everyone's attention, but the skinheads—for all the bovver and agro they and their successors provoke—have no better chance of survival or of leaving much permanent mark on the language than their fathers and uncles, the mods and rockers. How long shall we dig hippy pads? Even the somewhat greater currency that may be stimulated through advertisers incorporating such items into their slogans (cf. Leech 1966) is unlikely to make this an important source of linguistic change.

But there are longer-term trends whose effect can be noticeable even over a couple of decades. Again it is impossible to discuss them in isolation from the social trends they reflect. One is the urge towards analysis and elementalism. The Anglo-Saxons have been letting their hair down with a boldness and daring that have been gaining momentum throughout the present century, with much aiding and abetting from our neighbours across the seas. Nude shows, the pill, and pregnancy termination were naturally accompanied by equally radical changes in linguistic behaviour: the use of four-letter words by consenting broadcasters in public, and the like. After 70 years of movement in the same direction, there are still some polysyllabic fig-leaves that can be discarded if we want to get right down to the naked shame of everything. And there still seems to be some remaining steam behind the idea that it is therapeutic to revolt and useful to shock people out of their inhibitions. It is possible, therefore, that the trend in speech and writing, which already leaves us mystified as to why *The Rainbow* was prosecuted for obscenity in 1915, will give us further linguistic strip shows before 1990. But it seems to me equally likely that a reaction may set in before long, as people grow anxious about unending permissiveness —or get bored by it.

The social revolution of the past generation has already reversed the trend of Victorian, Edwardian and early BBC days towards the recognition of Oxbridge, Mayfair and the Court as the sole sources of a 'good accent'. In the wartime forties, the BBC tried to democratize what would have been more recently called its 'image' by having the Northern news read by a man with a slight Northern accent: protests from the north in favour of the 'Received Pronunciation', traditionally favoured as the upper class accent of Britain—or at any rate, of England. In the early fifties an Australian acquaintance of mine could not get a broadcasting job because listeners (including listeners in London) would resent her as some kind of Cockney and hence unfitted for the augustness of public address. In the past few years, we have come not merely to recognize an Australian accent as Australian but to accept it. Many of our daily newsreaders and news commentators are Australians, New Zealanders, South Africans, Canadians—not to mention Yorkshiremen and Cockneys: all freely and naturally using their native accents, while RP has taken its rightful place as just one of the acceptable ways of speaking English. And broadcasting even so is relatively selective so far as language use is concerned: at any rate, if we exclude the comedians and disc jockeys. Our more populous professions (especially teaching and medicine) are operated by men and women among whom RP speakers are almost certainly a minority; and immigration, internal migration, and the massive increase in the multiversity population have both accustomed our ears and adjusted our social antennae so as to comprehend and accept the accents of the Indian Subcontinent, West Africa, the West Indies, the industrial cities of our domestic provinces (still a prime source of cheap comedy, however), and the Antipodes.

Three components in this list are of special importance. The potential legacy of the coloured immigrant is most doubtful and everything depends upon current efforts (by the vast majority of our population) at genuine integration: if these are successful, the legacy is likely to be small since the generation born in Britain adopt the English around them and the idiom of their parents will disappear. I decline to speculate on alternatives.

The second significant component I had in mind was the accent of industrial areas. Partly through a more rational social outlook but partly also through the salutary democratizing effect of pop groups like the Beatles (if it be allowed that there are pop groups like the Beatles), relatively unconscious and unaffected adoption of regionalisms has taken place at a notable rate during the past decade ('gear', for example) and although many instances are in the slang range and therefore ephemeral, the trend they represent seems likely to leave its mark on the language.

Thirdly, and I think most significant of all, there is the new impact of Antipodean English. Having changed within a generation from a remote area of small political influence and almost no linguistic contact with Europe or North America, Australia (and to a lesser extent New Zealand) has projected itself as a political and economic force, and sprayed the cultural centres of the northern hemisphere with eager, confident young intellectuals who charm hosts and colleagues with a vivid but cultivated variety of English (cf. Turner 1966). I believe that Australia has already joined the United States as the predominant source of linguistic influence on British English. Very much in second place, but. And the reader's probable surprise at this Antipodean use of 'but' reminds us that we are very much more susceptible to vocabulary influence (*kangaroo*, *sheila*) than to grammatical.

Very much in second place. We must be in no doubt that the linguistic centre of gravity for the English-speaking world remains in the place it has securely occupied for a good many decades, and that it will remain in North America as we pass beyond our particular twenty-year span and into the twenty-first century. Specifically, the United States, of course. But as Canadian political and economic power develops, the source of linguistic influence may well increasingly spread north, though the virtual lack of a linguistic frontier at the forty-ninth parallel (this conveniently leaves Quebec out of account) makes the qualification largely academic. Grosvenor Square links the two countries in London and gives ironic assurance that Mayfair will still be a centre of influential language. Everyday English will continue to be freely expanded from American English and 'French fries' and 'campus' will be joined in the 1970's and 1980's by hundreds of other examples. The English of whole new areas of activity derives solidly from America: not merely the sinister trends in warfare such as 'defoliant' and 'overkill', but the language of factory automation, space exploration, and computer science (which has provided British English with a curious contrast between 'program' and 'programme' to parallel older doublets like 'flour' and 'flower', 'metal' and 'mettle'). In fact, much of the recent impact of continental languages such as German has been by a roundabout route involving a double crossing of the Atlantic. The 'dumb' that goes with blondes who are far from mute is an Americanism deriving from the German adjective *dumm*, and the 'fresh' that also goes with blondes is based on the German *frech*. The influence of Yiddish—as in 'O.K. by me'—is similarly exerted chiefly through American English and will probably go on increasing (cf. Rosten 1970).

The polysyllables of new learning often tell a similar story: elements from the culture of Greece and Rome are packaged and processed in the New World and re-exported to Britain and Europe. Indeed the plethora of opaque coinages like 'ergonomics' or 'autobibliography' is a fair indicator of what the future holds. Though more and more of them are coming to know small Latin and less Greek, English speakers have in no way lost their ability to form new words involving classical elements—or their enthusiasm for such neologisms. My mention earlier of the 20th-century trend towards brute Anglo-Saxon directness of language should not allow us to ignore the steady persistence of the longer-term trend to move from the native to the more resounding foreign and learned expression. A heart attack now seems less of a killer than coronary thrombosis, and who would have a sore throat when he can have streptococcal septicaemia? English may be expected to go still further along this painful road in the next twenty years.

Even so, I think it is the trend away from circumlocution and towards the colloquial and native models that is more likely to characterize new expression for the remainder of the century. It is of some significance that in two prestigious areas of scientific progress (computation and electronics), the developing language has stridently echoed the backroom lab rather than the Academy of Science: one thinks of 'input', 'output', 'store', 'drum', 'hardware', 'woofer', 'tweeter' and 'rumble'. This would seem to be in line with the movement away from formality towards a more casual and personal style in political rhetoric or the language of non-statutory official communications; away from the obscure and intellectual in religious language, too. Perhaps we might say that all this represents a tendency to increase the scope of what Crystal and Davy (1969) refer to as the 'common core': even though new specialist varieties of English (space communication, for example) will continue to emerge, we may expect to see less sharp distinctions between the language used in different activities and on different occasions. It may come to seem increasingly pompous to write characteristically 'scientific' English or make characteristically 'ministerial' speeches.

If so, it will be in line with my reason for all but ignoring one further type of change that English is likely to see: the continued emergence of new and additional 'standard Englishes', especially no doubt in the Antipodes and Southern Africa but also in Ireland, the Caribbean, and possibly also in areas such as India where English is a second rather than a native language. Such developments will reflect new political and cultural independence and self-respect, and they will be of major significance in the history of English as a whole. I do not adduce them as important in the context of the present paper for two reasons. First, insofar as the new standards are different from British English, they will not for that reason have any appreciable influence on changing the English of Britain. Secondly, self-assurance of the new standards seems to be showing itself in the avoidance of difference for difference's sake. In other words, English as a world language is reacting to important centripetal influences strictly analogous to those I have been predicting for English as a European language.

REFERENCES

D. Crystal and D. Davy, *Investigating English Style* (London, 1969), p. 150.

O. Jespersen, *Efficiency in Linguistic Change* (Copenhagen, 1941).

G. N. Leech, *English in Advertising* (London, 1966), p. 78.

L. Rosten, *The Joys of Yiddish* (London, 1970).

V. Tauli, *Introduction to a Theory of Language Planning* (Uppsala, 1968).

G. W. Turner, *The English Language in Australia and New Zealand* (London, 1966).

8 On Conceptions of good Grammar

My title is not merely unattractive: it is misleading. I am not going to talk so much about instances of good or bad grammar as about the various meanings of the word 'grammar' itself. Even so, I shall not be taking all the various meanings of 'grammar' into account. I shall be limiting the discussion to a set which have, I think, particular relevance for us as writers, scholars, and teachers of English. I shall invite you to consider seven such meanings, choosing the number seven not so much with the Seven Sages of Greece in mind, still less the Seven Wonders of the World, or the Seven Names of God; not even with the Seven Deadly Sins in mind, or the Seven Years War, though these are more tempting associations. A better analogue is the part of London known as the Seven Dials. The name was given to a point from which seven streets radiated (as they still do) and at which there was a sun-dial which had faces visible from all these directions.

The image is not unfitting for a word like 'grammar' whose meanings go out in sharply different directions, and it has the added advantage of giving me an excuse to borrow the story which underlies the title of Martin Joos's book, *The Five Clocks* (The Hague, 1962, p. 7). Ballyhough railway station in Ireland had two clocks which disagreed by some six minutes. When an irate traveller asked a porter what was the use of having two clocks if they didn't tell the same time, the porter replied, 'And what would we be wanting with two clocks if they told the same time?' I shall be claiming that we need the seven dials for grammar because they do not all tell the same time.

My starting-point is not, however, Ballyhough station but a leading article in the *Daily Telegraph* ten years ago which sparked off one of those recurrent high-temperature discussions that we have from time to time about the state of literacy among the younger generation. The leading article attributed the alleged

The Giff Edmonds Memorial Lecture read to the Royal Society of Literature on 15 June 1967.

decline in English usage to certain trends in modern educational theory and practice:

> as the attention given to 'modern subjects' has increased, the liberal arts have had to be proportionately squeezed. Perhaps there is little point in sighing for the days when all the arts were indeed liberal: but the needs of a technocratic age are no excuse for neglect of the plain, simple machinery of our mother tongue. . . The art of grammar was, after all, the traditional preoccupation of the grammar schools. Let them look to it. (31 August 1957.)

We shall not pause to wonder with what justification the writer thinks the machinery of our mother tongue is 'plain' and 'simple' or what he understands by 'liberal' when he wishes that the arts were still 'indeed liberal'. We must, however, take note that his weighty peroration uses 'grammar' in two distinct meanings in a single short sentence, the first being one that we shall explore here; the other (which is 'classical studies, especially Latin') being one we must otherwise ignore. Nor, I think, am I being unfair in picking on a technicality in the non-technical public press. Last year, the Incorporated Association of Assistant Masters issued the third edition of *The Teaching of English*, a work addressed to teachers in secondary schools, and we find a similar rhetorical use of the connection: 'All the boys and girls who come to grammar schools need some grammar' (Cambridge, 1966, p. 16).

But let us now look at the seven meanings which I should like to isolate for the purposes of our discussion today. I hope that each may be adequately both distinguished and illustrated in a single key sentence, and I also hope that the illustrations will show that all these meanings are current, common, and non-technical.

1. *Latin has a good deal of grammar, but English has hardly any.*

The first of these meanings is in many respects also the narrowest. It is the one that has given rise to the common collocation 'grammar and syntax', thus carrying the implication that syntax is not a part of grammar. Its implications, however, go far beyond this. Clearly, it is a meaning that has emerged from the traditional identification, already mentioned, of grammar with classical and especially Latin studies. If grammar once meant the learning of Latin, it is natural that it should also come to mean inflexions or accidence, since inflexions play such a dominant role in Latin and preoccupy the learner's attention for a large part of his studies. Since one effect of the post-Renaissance cult of the vernaculars was to see them as fashioned in Latin's image, it was equally natural that linguistic study of them should focus on features analogous to the dominant ones in Latin. And since there were fewer inflexions in English, there was less 'grammar' and the notion of English as an easy language, a simplified language, grew up. Nor, I must insist, is this a trivial matter of popular parlance but an idea of long-standing among our leading thinkers. Thus, Sir Philip Sidney, towards the end of his essay *The Apologie for Poetrie*, accepts the criticism that English has little grammar but claims that this is a point in its favour, 'beeing so easie of it selfe, and so voyd of those cumbersome differences of Cases, Genders, Moodes, and Tenses, which I thinke was a peece of the Tower of *Babilons* curse'. Again, in his *Lectures on the English Language*, published a century ago, we find George Marsh referring to English as 'having no grammar', and so powerful did this belief become that few ever challenged the claims for the simplicity of Basic English that Ogden and Richards made on precisely these grounds.[1]

The second meaning that we should distinguish seems very similar to the first and indeed there are important connections:

2. *French has a good logical grammar but English is full of irregularities and idioms.*

Here again we are concerned with an informal comparison of two languages and here again English is regarded as being somehow deficient. But this time a good deal more than inflexions seems to be at issue, and you may agree that the mention of 'logic' in the first half of the illustrative sentence, and of 'idiom' in the second, shifts the emphasis rather to syntax. In other words, if 'grammar' in the first of our meanings excludes syntax, this second meaning tends if anything to exclude the inflexions with which the first meaning was virtually identified.

Our second example raises, however, more important issues than this shift of emphasis. I think it is important to realize that whereas, given a Latin-orientated cultural history, the first meaning would seem true and obvious to the speaker of any language at all, this second meaning will seem most true and obvious to a native speaker of English. This is not a matter of the Anglo-Saxon sport of criticizing one's own institutions. It is a result of the fact that the native speaker learns the rules of his own language by a process which, although we know almost nothing about it, is quite different from and much less conscious than his way of learning a foreign language. This has the paradoxical effect that, while the native language remains the only language that most of us can use effortlessly, it is the *foreign* language whose rules we—in some sense—'know' and can repeat or explain. And since we find ourselves so often unable to explain to a foreigner or our own children the rules for a given construction, it readily seems to us that this is because—unlike the foreign language we have been laboriously taught—English has little regularity but much idiom. Testing this assertion is somewhat complicated by the educational and cultural background of an informant (notably in connection with the third meaning which we shall come to presently), but it is nevertheless quite easy to demonstrate the matter by asking a German tourist who is not a teacher of German to explain the rule about verbs with separable prefixes. He is quite likely to have greater difficulty doing so than an English boy preparing for 'O' Level German, and he is quite likely to end up with an apologetic smile saying that it is just idiomatic. Even, indeed, the points at which a native speaker feels there is complete regularity, he may find himself unable to state the rules and may therefore feel that there are none or only trivial, irrelevant, and self-evident ones. It is this situation which makes it difficult for the native English student to use even so excellent a book as the *Handbook of English Grammar* of R. W. Zandvoort (London, 1957), in the very first paragraph of which the third person singular present of English regular verbs is explained as follows:

> [iz] is used after stems ending in a sibilant, [z] in other cases, except after breathed consonants, [s] after breathed consonants, except sibilants.

This accounts admirably for the difference between *he passes*, *he calls*, *he waits*, but is relevant only for the foreign learner; no native speaker, however young, is aware of any difference to be accounted for and that which needs no rules cannot easily be felt to have any.

We may now cautiously approach the third of our meanings, the illustrative sentence for which is as follows:

3. *French has a good, well-defined grammar but in English you're free to speak as you like.*

It will at once be clear why we need to be cautious at this point; the third meaning can easily be confused with the second that we have already considered, for the very good reason that English speakers usually make statements involving meaning (2) about those languages, such as French or Spanish or Italian, for which meaning (3) is also applicable. With meaning (3), that is, we are concerned with the notion of an officially institutionalized grammar by a national academy. What the Swedes call *språkvård* and the Germans *Sprachpflege* may have small actual effect on linguistic usage, and the effect certainly varies from country to country, but one important effect is seen in the educational system. Where a language academy exists, there is usually a strong tradition for an insistent teaching of the rules, so that young Frenchmen at least usually have a fair knowledge of the rules they break. Since this is so, it tends to perpetuate the false belief that we considered when we looked at the second meaning, namely, that every language has firm rules except English. It is significant that the Swedish and German words that I have just used cannot easily be translated into English; it is significant that the Society for Pure English remained a small and rather esoteric group without official backing and that it passed quietly out of existence some twenty years ago. We probably could not sustain a regular feature on such matters in the public press analogous to Robert le Bidois's *La Défense de la langue française* in *Le Monde*, and it would sound either facetious or jingoistic if it were called 'The Defence of English.' In the years around 1700, of course, the idea would have seemed more natural. In the context of the formation of the continental academies, numerous moves in this direction were made in England. If Swift had had his way, we might well have had a word today for *Sprachpflege*, and the word might have been' 'ascertainment'. It will be recalled that Swift's famous *Proposal* of 1712 listed among the imperfections of English 'that in many instances it offends against every part of grammar'.[2]

The proposal was never adopted and to this day we lack the appeal to authority which is our third meaning of 'grammar'. While there is a strong popular tradition (its justification need not concern us) for appealing to '*the* dictionary' to prove whether or not a disputed word warrants the triumphant rejection, 'There's no such word', we cannot make a comparable appeal to '*the* grammar'. Some individual grammarians have come close to remedying the deficiency—Fowler in our own time, Latham a century ago, and, above all, Lindley Murray at the close of the eighteenth century. Indeed, the latter's *English Grammar* of 1795 defines his work in terms which clearly identify his concept of grammar with the meaning under discussion: 'the art of speaking and writing the English language with propriety.'

But with individual grammarians, we have in fact arrived at our fourth meaning:

4. *Jespersen wrote a good grammar but Nesfield's is boring.*

When we ask questions like 'Have you a Bible?' or 'Have you a Shakespeare?', we mean 'Have you a copy of the unchanging body of writing that we call "the Bible"?' (~ 'that comprises the the work of Shakespeare?'). As I indicated above, there is a

similar feeling for a body of unchanging data called 'the dictionary', and I suspect that when people say 'Have you a dictionary?'
they often mean analogously 'Have you a copy of "the" dictionary?' We need have no such suspicions about the indefinite article
with 'grammar', and as our example of the fourth meaning indi-
cates, we are all thoroughly used to subjecting grammars to the
sceptical appraisal that we adopt also for cookery books. Nor is
the connection between grammars and cookbooks entirely inappropriate: the authors of both types of work are felt alike to begin
with a mass of unstructured raw data and at their will they produce
recipes for various occasions which we may like or dislike according to taste.

Thus, although meanings (3) and (4) resemble each other in
referring to a codification of the rules for a particular language,
they differ sharply in the degree of authority implied. And there
are other differences which likewise spring from the individuality
of the codification referred to with meaning (4). Some grammars
are written for mature scholars, some are written for school-
children; some are written for foreign learners, some for native
speakers; some have the aim of giving the history of every construction, some are concerned only with the contemporary language. All these purposes result in sharply different organizations
of what might be called 'the same' material. But there are still
further ramifications to what 'grammar' in this fourth sense may
mean. Where a 200-page grammar of modern French may be
expected to deal almost exclusively with syntax and a 200-page
grammar of Latin divide its attention between inflexions and
syntax, a grammar of Old English or Old High German may
with equal confidence be expected to present matter of an entirely
different kind. In these latter cases, more than half the space is
likely to be devoted to historical phonology, tracing the evolution
of the vowels and consonants from Proto-Germanic or even Indo-
European, with the bulk of the remainder devoted to a *non*-
historical presentation of the inflexions; there may be nothing on
the syntactical end of the grammatical spectrum at all.

The grammars in this fourth sense will also vary according to
the grammatical theory embraced by their authors, and this brings
us to the next meaning that we have to consider:

5. *Chomsky has devised a good grammar, but traditional
   grammar is unenlightening.*

This is the most abstract, elusive, and (in C. S. Lewis's[3] sense)
'dangerous' meaning that we have to consider. Since we are here
concerned with the fundamental theories informing approaches
to the study of language, the understanding of discussions involv-

ing this use of the word 'grammar' not merely requires that we understand the nature of the relation between a theory and the material it seeks to explicate: it requires also a fair degree of acquaintance with the specific theories. It goes without saying that the second of these conditions is quite often unfulfilled and so it would seem, all too frequently, is the first.

The complexity of the problem may be clearer if we consider an example. Let us suppose that we are trying to compare an observation on 'grammar' in sense (5) in the work of the late Professor W. J. Entwistle of Oxford with an observation on 'grammar', also in sense (5) in the work of Professor R. B. Lees of Illinois. The effort to relate the two observations requires us to know and, if possible, to take account of the sharply different theories informing the two observations. To Entwistle, grammar is 'the construction placed by mind on the unorganized materials of speech. . . That grammar is arbitrary seems to become evident as we consider opposite ways of effecting the same end. No one device can be deemed more natural than another' (*Aspects of Language*, London, 1953, p. 145). To Lees, grammar is seen as 'a theory which will generate all and only grammatical sentences by means of naturally chosen, maximally simple, unrepeated rules' (*Language*, 33, 1957, p. 389). The one is imposing an arbitrary, consciously unnatural order on chaos; the other is simulating the natural creative potentiality in the human linguistic mechanism. It may well be as difficult to relate statements by these two scholars as it is to relate the work of a geologist to that of an architect. Yet this is the problem that confronts us—all the more frightening for being unacknowledged—when we find teachers eager to reject 'traditional grammar' and to replace it by 'the new grammar'. On the one hand, there is being rejected an approach whose 2,000-year-old theoretical basis is quite possibly not understood: that is to say, even if one agreed with the rejection one cannot easily be sure one is agreeing with the motives for rejection. On the other hand, there is not one new grammar but many (some of them very old but writ new) and they have many different aims. In other words, it may be right to discontinue geology and to study architecture in its place, but we must not propose such a change under the impression that architecture is merely an improved form of geology.

It is with some relief that we turn to the sixth meaning of 'grammar' which is decidedly easier to understand:

6. *John uses good grammar, but his spelling is awful.*

In juxtaposing the most difficult and theoretical meaning with the easiest and most practical (as well as probably the most common),

I am of course leading up to a full realization of the confusion that conceptions of 'good grammar' can produce. But for the present let us notice two aspects of this sixth sense. In the first place, it seems worth noting that in the most ordinary and non-technical discourse people clearly conceive of 'good grammar' as having a relatively well-defined reference within the totality of linguistic usage such that it certainly excludes spelling and pronunciation and probably with equal definiteness excludes use of vocabulary items and the meaning of words as well. If a child is found using *interloper* where he should be using *interpreter*, no one is likely to say that this is bad grammar. In the second place, let us consider whether even this sixth meaning of grammar is as easy to understand as we thought. If we carefully exclude from our minds the earlier senses (particularly the fourth), then we may agree that

6a. *John has a good knowledge of grammar*

refers to sentence structure, sequence of tenses, case, number, and the like, whether it is expanded as

6b. *John has a good knowledge of grammar and his sentences are very shapely*

or as

6c. *John has a good knowledge of grammar but he can't write correct English.*

It may well be objected that the apparent incompatibility is occasioned by the ambiguity of 'knowledge' rather than the ambiguity of 'grammar', and I would be prepared to agree. But the fact remains that, to the extent that (6b) and (6c) are sensible, meaningful sentences, they show that it is possible to conceive of a knowledge of grammar which informs or preconditions our use of a language, and a knowledge of the same grammatical data that exists independently of our ability to use the language. We may notice in this connection that it would make sense to say of an English child

6d. *He knows no grammar but he speaks correct English*

but not to say

6e. *He knows no grammar but he speaks correct French.*

This is tantamount to admitting that the grammatical data we are discussing when we use 'grammar' in the sixth meaning are part of a natural ability in relation to the native language, and that, unlike the grammatical data of a foreign language, the teacher's task is only to make the learner aware of what he knows already.

In speaking of the teacher's task, we have arrived at 'grammar' as a curricular subject, our seventh and final sense:

7. *English grammar is good but I hate arithmetic.*

In introducing the sixth meaning, I said it was probably the commonest and least technical, and if I am right in feeling that this seventh meaning is almost as common and as commonplace, we might well expect a good deal of direct correspondence between them—especially as both so obviously share the aura of the schoolroom. But in fact we find here a source of fresh confusion. It will be recalled that the sixth meaning clearly excluded spelling, pronunciation, vocabulary, and so on. Curiously perhaps (and certainly unfortunately), there are no similar limits on 'grammar' as a subject. Let me quote again from the 1966 edition of the I.A.A.M. handbook on *The Teaching of English*:

> The aim of a grammar lesson . . . is to create an interest in words . . . Investigation into their origin and meaning is nearly always popular and useful. Here the appeal is mainly historical. More exciting is the attack on neologisms, which takes us straight into such splendid fields as American English, slang, modern science . . . Latin and Greek roots . . . English spelling . . . the traditional rules for pronunciation . . . (pp. 15–16).

However 'exciting' and 'splendid' these activities may be, they are very much wider and more varied than meaning (6) would lead us to expect: the 'good grammar' that John is taught by no means corresponds to the 'good grammar' that John is judged to know or use. So it is that, within the same classroom, it makes sense to utter both sentence (6) and also

7a. *Grammar is good when it consists of spelling-bees.*

Splendid and exciting it undoubtedly is, but let it be perfectly clear to us all that it is not 'grammar' in any of the six earlier senses that we have examined.

Let us now turn back to our starting-point, the *Daily Telegraph* leading article. What is it that this article is seeking to reinstate in schools? Is it the same as what Mr David Holbrook has recently referred to as 'the old grammar grind?'[4] And if it is, why should anyone want to reintroduce something of which Holbrook so resoundingly disapproves? It surely cannot be that Holbrook would call an 'old grind' what the Incorporated Association of Assistant Masters calls 'splendid' and 'exciting'. We have seen of course that there are several points at which confusion can arise through the sharply different meanings possessed by the word 'grammar' and that there are other points (for example, meaning (1) itself) at which prejudice can grow up against the idea of teaching English grammar. What greater waste of time is conceivable?

Confusion is worse confounded, however, when we look at some of the ways in which 'the art of grammar' is actually handled in schools. The Educational Institute of Scotland in 1939 issued a statement on *The Junior Secondary School*, in which it was claimed that 'The function of grammar [our meaning seven, of course] is to assist pupils to read with understanding and to speak and write correctly' [i.e. to acquire good grammar in meaning six]; it is, in short, 'a practical aid to composition'. We should note that it is an untested assumption that 'grammar' in meaning seven can lead to the acquisition of 'grammar' in meaning six, and we need not be surprised that it remains an assumption when we hear how 'grammar' seven is taught in the very schools that come within the Institute's purview. W. J. Macauley has told us[5] of a 'typical scheme of work to be covered in the primary school' as 'used in Glasgow'. Daily classes of about half an hour are as follows: at the age of $7\frac{1}{2}$ years, pupils have lessons on the noun and the verb, singular and plural number; at 8 the study of adjectives is added; at $8\frac{1}{2}$ personal pronouns and the tenses of verbs. How children have managed with verbs but no tenses for a whole year is unexplained. Despite this, says Macauley, teachers complain that 'pupils entering the secondary school appear to show a complete lack of understanding of even the terms of grammar'. That is, not only is composition presumably unaided but pupils have not even acquired the patter implied in sentence (6c). And in case this example suggests that the situation is especially deplorable in Scotland, let me just quote from the English Association's publication of 1946, *The Teaching of English in Schools*, in which it is stated that 'the more formal parts of grammar could, in view of their simplicity in English, be mastered between the ages of 10 and 12'. If 'grammar' is being used in senses one or two, then we have seen that it is not 'simple' for English but that it would, of course, have indeed been mastered by the age of 10; so there is nothing to teach in any case. If it is being used in sense seven (the only other possibility), then we have seen from the Scottish experiences that it is unlikely to be learnt by the age of 12 and that its usefulness would be highly questionable even if it were.

It is not part of my purpose today to say in what sense—if any —grammar should be 'looked to' in grammar schools, but it occurs to me that grammar-school pupils could do worse than be taught to understand the many ways in which the word 'grammar' is used in discourse about language. In particular, since every normal person seems to have a keen interest in speculating about the nature of his own language, it might be of special interest to help people to understand meanings two, four, and five, and the relation between them. Thus it is interesting (and apparently not obvious) that every language is an elaborate code of rules, and every one to a greater or lesser extent a different code. This is meaning two, and further consideration of it (by means, for example, of sentence 2) brings home to us the subjective apprehension that the codes are different in kind—notably that the code of one's native language is very differently apprehended from the code of a language that we learn as a foreign language. And this leads us to consider the presumably very different learning mechanisms that are involved, differing perhaps more in terms of the age at which we learn the native language than in terms of the method ('direct', 'translation', etc.) by which we learn a foreign language.

These different codes invite the construction of theories to account for language rules, the best way to describe them, the best way to regard their relationship to each other and to the rest of human behaviour. This is grammar in sense five. And finally, we come to applications of a grammar in sense five to a grammar in sense two in order to produce a grammar in sense four—a book which sets out the code of a particular language, setting it out, that is, in a form that is quite different from the code in its natural state (as the language itself) and made interestingly accessible for intellectual examination as distinct from practical use.

The convincingness of such a three-way relationship between senses two, four, and five may be increased by comparing a projected (and perhaps more readily recognizable) three-way relationship in the field of vocabulary. It probably requires little effort to realize that every language has its own vocabulary, seen as a large stock of separate names for things and qualities and activities, and that every language's word stock is to a greater or lesser degree independent of every other language's. This corresponds to grammar in sense two. Now as soon as we start cataloguing the wordstock, we realize we have to think of what exactly a word is, what we are going to call a word for our cataloguing purposes: is *goodbye* or *how do you do* a word because *cheerio* and *hello* seem to be? But then what about *good night*? How many words are there in *Thank you, il y a, gas stove, railway station refreshment room, Eintrittsgeld*? And there are other considerations: should my catalogue give the history of the words, their pronunciation, their meaning? Should it try to include everything like the latest big *Webster* or try to be selective like the latest *Concise Oxford*? These theoretical matters are clearly analogous to and perhaps valuable in explaining grammar in sense five. And then finally there are the catalogues themselves which make the vocabulary accessible, however oddly abstracted from the language and even more oddly ordered: the catalogues that we call dictionaries and which bring together the theory (as in 'grammar five') with the material of the specific language (as in 'grammar two') to form a description after the manner of 'grammar four'.

It is not claimed that any such organization of our conceptions of grammar or other aspects of linguistic form will help the *Daily Telegraph* to remedy the nation's bad grammar. But at least it may direct our attention (and that of our pupils) towards the nature of good grammar itself.

NOTES

1. See, however, Ifor Evans, *The Use of English* (2nd ed., London, 1966), especially pp. 54 ff.
2. For a meticulous analysis of this use of 'grammar', see I. A. Richards, *Interpretation in Teaching* (London, 1938), pp. 212 ff.
3. Cf. *Studies in Words* (Cambridge, 1960), pp. 12 ff.
4. *The Exploring Word* (Cambridge, 1967), p. 182.
5. *British Journal of Educational Psychology*, 17 (1947).

9 The Toils of Fowler and Moral Gowers

I

One hundred years ago today[1] was born a man whose name achieved the moderately rare distinction of becoming a household word. 'What does it say in Fowler?' is not of course as common an appeal as 'What does it say in the Dictionary?', but the two imply a similar trust as in an oracle, erecting a mystical authority and investing it in a single volume. In the case of 'Fowler', the abstraction process goes further, singling out one Fowler from the two brothers and one work from among the considerable output that the elder, Henry Watson Fowler, has to his credit. This is something of a pity for at least two reasons. In the first place, as Henry constantly and perhaps overgenerously insisted, much of the Fowler work was jointly conceived and executed by the two brothers, notably the fine but nowadays rather neglected *King's English* of 1906, and the first edition of the *Concise Oxford Dictionary*. Even *Modern English Usage* was begun in consultation with Frank, though written without his actual participation and published some years after his death. In the second place, the close tying in the public mind of Fowler and a single book, *Modern English Usage*, is to be regretted because this is to ignore his other work and to invite a judgment of his achievement on the basis of this one alone. Not that one would very much want to bring into the reckoning his volumes of essays, *If Wishes Were Horses*, and *Some Comparative Values*, though some of the pieces in these are pretty enough. But it is his lexicographical work as a whole that needs to be considered.

Of him, *The Times Literary Supplement* wrote over thirty years ago, 'a man could hardly face the toils of dictionary-making unless he had some special zest'. Fowler had that special zest in abundance, and indeed when he was over 70, he was so ready for further labours as to embark on the ten-year programme required to write the *Quarto Oxford Dictionary*. It was in dictionary work that his considerable special gifts could be exercised to best advantage: his learning and wide reading, his incisive clarity, his love of logic, his legal flair for definition and categorization, his devotion to the humdrum tasks of compiling and labelling,—even his wit. (The definition of the word *wing* in the *Concise Oxford Dictionary*, for instance, begins 'One of the limbs or organs by which the flight of a bird, bat, insect, angel etc is effected'.) And by the same token, dictionary work prevented him from giving rein to those qualities in him which were—relatively speaking—his vices: prolixity, prejudice, dogmatism, and complex logic-chopping as he ensnared an offending locution. These were his other toils. Nor does one need to apologize for the pun: he took pride and pleasure in a *Times* leader not long before his death entitled 'The Fowler's Net'.

Does this mean, then, that we remember Fowler for the wrong book? Well, not altogether. It must be noted that the full title of this book is *A Dictionary of Modern English Usage*, and that many of its entries are indeed such stuff as good dictionaries are made on. One thinks of numerous lexical matters like the distinguishing of near-synonyms, the explication of words frequently misunderstood or confused, and the discussion of spelling, stressing and pronunciation in relation to individual words. One might cite as an example his article on *liberal* which constitutes a valuable essay on the meaning of the word as applied to education. It is in such articles—and they are very many—that the abiding value of the book rests. Yet even on these strictly lexical matters we all too frequently see the qualities which at once mar the book and give it the distinctive character and appeal that contributes to its having sold half a million copies and account for its present annual sale of twenty thousand. The article on *meticulous* begins 'What is the strange charm that makes this wicked word irresistible to the British journalist?', the first of a string of six rhetorical questions, a device for commentary not favoured in modern lexicographical practice. And although *Modern English Usage* gives no prefatory warning on this point, Fowler makes clear elsewhere (in a Society for Pure English *Tract* of 1927) that his aim is not that of an observer telling people 'what they do' but that of a moralizer telling them 'what he thinks they ought to do'. Not for him the modest role of describer, played with ostentatious diffidence by his structuralist contemporaries.

Having assumed the teacher's gown, he will not only give an objective account of the actual usage of *large, small, big, little, great, much*, so as to point out with admirable clarity the difference for us, but he will—when he disapproves of actual usage—condemn and outlaw words like *meticulous* and *banality*, as literary critics' words, pretentious and unnecessary, and will demonstrate with equal clarity and forthrightness what alternatives should be used. To this end, *coastal* is labelled 'regrettable', *bureaucrat* 'barbarous', and *speedometer* 'a monstrosity'. Much of which, as he regretfully acknowledges himself from time to time, is doomed to futility, even where the clarity of his argument is matched by soundness; and this is not always the case. Fowler tends to wrestle with no holds barred. His attack on the literary critics for using *meticulous* is based partly on the fact that the word is unnecessary since its functions are catered for by *scrupulous* and *punctilious* (a claim which will not stand examination even in the light of his own *Concise Oxford Dictionary*). And it is based partly on the fact that its English meaning does not match that of the corresponding Latin form (found only, as he says scornfully, 'in Plautus or somewhere'). Yet this is an attitude to correct meaning which he rightly rejects elsewhere in *Modern English Usage* itself.

But, rejected elsewhere or not, this appeal to a Latin base as a guide to English usage is something that affects more than his attack on *meticulous*: it underlies, one might say underlines, many of his pronouncements on grammar, undoubtedly the weakest feature in all his work. It was for this reason that I drew prime attention to his achievement as a lexicographer: he was no great grammarian, still less a scientific linguist in any of the modern senses applied to this variable profession. Yet many of the articles in *Modern English Usage*, as well as the title itself, invited judgment of him precisely *as* a grammarian, though any of a score of his major articles on grammar will clearly show his deficiencies in this field. The one on *Cases*, for instance, draws attention to the inadequacy of his analysis. The example *me and my mates likes ends* is supposed to show that the speaker had no use for the subject form *I*, though he presumably did not think that the same 'speaker' would add 'but me used to'. His reliance—as in this example—on literary evidence for spoken English, and his belief that it was feasible to change pronoun usage by some sort of intellectual agreement arrived at between the speakers of English, make it difficult to take his observations seriously. Moreover, in matters of grammar he operates with Shibboleths labelled 'strictly correct', which are quite distinct not only from the actual usage of good writers, but distinct even from the actual form being recommended by Fowler himself.

He feels strongly enough to describe *it's me* as 'a blunder' in one place, though elsewhere with rather more sense of proportion he lets it pass as 'a lapse of no importance'; he sticks out for *pacificist* though admitting that *pacifist* is thoroughly established; logic —always a favourite weapon in Fowler's grammatical armoury, and as devastating as it was inappropriate—induces him to

condemn *all men do not speak German* even while describing it as
'natural and idiomatic English'. A rational approach to grammar
of course, can lead to other difficulties, including the rationalizer's
difficulty of practising what he preaches. Thus, although at one
place (p. 537) he deprecates the *s* genitive in usages like 'the
narrative's charm', he has earlier fallen into the practice himself
with 'the termination's capabilities' (p. 5) and 'the sentence's
structure' (p. 6). He recommends us to say *Could you tell me what
the time is?* while in the same breath saying that nevertheless it
would be 'strictly correct' to say 'Could you tell me what the time
was?'—an example, incidentally, of the inadequacy of his analytic
powers as a grammarian in reckoning *could* as a past tense in
such instances.

   This observation is astonishingly retained intact in a recent
revision of the book by Margaret Nicholson, entitled *A Dictionary of American English Usage* (1957), as well of course as in all
intermediate editions and reprints. Its retention is the more
astonishing in that it was an example which particularly shocked a
reviewer of the first edition of 1926 and provoked the outburst:
'This is the sort of grammar writing which one would hardly
expect'. It is in fact worth making the point, perhaps, that our
disapproval of his approach is not just wisdom after the event, the
1950's looking back more in pity than in anger at the 20's. Most
serious reviewers made all these criticisms in 1926 and 1927. It was
not only the great Dutch grammarian Kruisinga in a peevish and
sarcastic article who said the home truths: a more objective review in the German periodical *Englische Studien* listed a dozen
standard monographs, an acquaintance with which would have
saved Fowler from many of the fallacies that nevertheless went
uncorrected.

   But if he took little notice of *most* critics, there is plenty of
evidence in his correspondence and published work alike to show
that the strictures of Otto Jespersen really struck home. In a reply
published in 1927 from which I have already quoted, Fowler gives
a clearer statement of his grammatical principles than anywhere
else. He rejects Jespersen's suggestion that Latin grammar ought
to apply only to Latin, and insists on the standards and rules of
Latin grammar being considered applicable to English whenever
they can be possibly relevant. We need not pay too serious attention to his sarcastic scorn for Jespersen's alternative and superbly
original analyses: there is evidence that he was less at ease in this
discussion with his most formidable professional opponent than
in his self-confident logic-chopping with, say, A. A. Milne in the
correspondence columns of *The Times Literary Supplement*. But I
do not think we can similarly dismiss this clear statement about

the universality and primacy of Latin grammar. Despite all our affection for Fowler, we cannot but recognize these defects in his approach as utterly gross when we reflect that books in his own time not only by Jespersen but by Wyld, Bloomfield, Sapir and others could have developed in him a maturer and more sophisticated approach; when we reflect too that here he was in 1927 defending views that had been completely discredited by Henry Sweet fifty years earlier in such papers as 'Words, Logic and Grammar' (*Transactions of the Philological Society*) and rarely advanced thereafter by serious (as opposed to amateur) grammarians; and when we reflect that Sweet's splendid and still unequalled *New English Grammar* had been published a decade before ever the Fowler brothers conceived the idea in 1911 of writing *Modern English Usage*.

Yet the reader of *Modern English Usage* cannot even depend on Fowler as being a classic representative of the conservative authoritarian grammarian, the latter day version of the eighteenth-century prescriptivist and universal grammarian whom he so much resembles. One would welcome such a representative, but he is not one. His attitude to pronunciation for instance is curiously 'enlightened' and liberal—even permissive: speak like your neighbours, even if this means ignoring spelling, and rhyming *forehead* and *clothes* with *horrid* and *nose*. In grammar too, he is frequently daring and quite ready to support what the more timid or the more traditional condemn. He defends *different to* against those who say that it ought to be *different from*, and indeed he has two articles on what he calls *fetishes* and *superstitions* where similar bêtes noires are clothed in the whitest fleece— the split infinitive for instance. No, we cannot depend on the Fowler of *Modern English Usage* to give us either an objective account of what Modern English Usage is, or a representative summary of what the Latin-dominated traditionalists would have it be. *Modern English Usage* is personal: it *is* Fowler. And in this no doubt lies some of its perennial appeal. Fowler, the critics' critic, with a keen eye for the illogical, the absurd, the ugly, the pretentious, with a keen wit and ready pen that is able to expose these things and indeed debunk almost any treasured habit of the pompous.

It is this personal approach that gives the book those odd characteristics which enhance it while at the same time detracting from it as a reference work. Thus I have praised Fowler above as a lexicographer and praised *Modern English Usage* in so far as it dealt with lexical matters. But clearly, the dictionary presentation is unequal to the type of personal reflection that Fowler wants to offer, and one result is the interspersing of articles which have reasonable and self-evident headings with full-length essays which although also integrated into the alphabetical scheme have titles that simply cannot lend themselves to ready reference. A reader, after all, has to know his 740 pages of Fowler pretty well before it becomes automatic to seek guidance on constructing a sentence like 'Either he did or did not' under the heading *Unequal Yokefellows*, the appropriateness of which is only apparent on reading the article itself. This is also true of such entries as *Cannibalism* and *Swapping Horses*. Alternatively, if you discover—as you inevitably do—information which is highly useful, you close the book infuriatingly aware that you may never be able to find it again. In many respects, the earlier book *The King's English* is much more satisfactory for the purpose of reference, with its chapter-by-chapter construction and greatly superior index. But on the other hand *The King's English* could not provide Fowler with the freedom to write that myriad of independent, disconnected essays, long and short, on all kinds of topics, which give *Modern English Usage* the distinctive charm almost of a commonplace book.

When *Modern English Usage* first appeared, it was suggested that after fifty years, in 1976, someone ought to investigate the influence exerted by the book. That time is not yet and so fortunately such an immensely difficult task need not be attempted. Yet the present occasion does seem to call for some kind of appraisal, however imprecise and tentative, of the impact that Fowler has had. And here I think, one can sharply distinguish his influence in *detail* from his influence in *principle*. In detail—that is, in his recommendations about specific words and locutions—his influence would seem to be very slight indeed. True, I think that cats *can* effect an entrance nowadays unaccompanied by an allusion to 'harmless necessary', but I doubt whether this is a result of our studying Fowler's section on 'Hackneyed Phrases'. *Meticulous*, *coastal* and of course *bureaucrats* thrive, despite Fowler, and so do 'without the people minding', 'it's me', and 'it looks as if we are winning' (which Fowler condemns as an illiteracy). Equally, despite Fowler's approval of such points, people still object to the use of *different to* and more people say *forehead* than the laissez-faire [forid] that he blessed: and many of us would prefer to risk being ridiculed as genteel rather than speak of our *bellies*.

Yet in principle, his influence is perhaps quite extensive. We are probably more self-critical in the use of hackneyed phrases, hyphens, gallicisms, and even Unequal Yokefellows and Cannibalisms than the first readers of *The King's English* and *Modern English Usage*. The Fowler brothers, and particularly the man whose anniversary we are remembering, heightened the sense of style and personal responsibility for expression among writers in the English-speaking world. As well as having respectable antecedents in the eighteenth century themselves, they were the true begetters of a noble line of men who have further sharpened our awareness of these things—Alan Herbert, Ivor Brown, Eric Partridge and Ernest Gowers, to mention only a few. Yet even where the influence has been positive, its worth may still be called in question: as the edition of 1957 shows, the aura of authority around the name of Fowler has led to the perpetuation of such notions as 'strictly correct' which are as befogged and misleading now (if no longer as inhibiting) as they were recognized to be before ever the Fowlers put pen to paper.

II

The new *Modern English Usage*[2] has deserved the widespread and generally approbatory notices that it has received. 'After 40 years,' a common theme has been, 'it was time to take a fresh look at the English language,' and several reviewers have made explicit some of the assumptions underlying this theme. At least three are in fact questionable. The first is that English has changed radically in the past 40 years, and this is true almost only in respect of rather peripheral features. There are certainly thousands of new words, but the regularly revised conventional dictionaries take care of *radar*, *cosmonauts*, and the like; for the rest, the newness is each year's crop of ephemera, whether slang or the fashionable 'OK' word like *committed* or *escalate*. The majority of the problems of style or grammar or spelling which drive us quailing into the Fowler's net are much the same now as they were in 1926—or 1826. The second assumption is that English usage was described and its problems definitively solved by Fowler 40 years ago. There is less excuse for this assumption than for the previous one: it is glaringly false, as the really great grammarians of English— Jespersen and Kruisinga—devastatingly and acidly explained in the twenties. The third assumption is the least justifiable of all: that, being handed an authoritative but ageing account of a sup- posedly much-changed language, Sir Ernest Gowers has turned it into an authoritative account of English usage today.

Let it be understood that challenging this last assumption is no criticism of Gowers. If anyone is capable of an informed synoptic view of English, it is he. If there had been a sound description of English 40 years old, he could indeed have provided the slight but delicately difficult revision necessary to bring it up to date. But there was not: there was Fowler. And the Clarendon Press's brief to Sir Ernest was not to produce a new account of English usage but to produce a new edition of Fowler in such a way as to do 'what Fowler himself might have done'. Acknowledging Fowler's idiosyncrasies, his prolixity, his reliance on instinct and not on observation or linguistic theory, Sir Ernest in consequence tells us that 'no attempt has been made to convert the instinctive grammatical moralizer into anything else'; that he has 'been chary of making any substantial alterations'; that he has, in short, avoided 'any sacrifice of Fowleresque flavour'.

With this policy I am in full sympathy. However misleading he has been to the puzzled foreign learner taking too literally the title *Modern English Usage*, Fowler has been excellent value to the millions of native English speakers throughout the world who have been able to read into his title the subliminal gloss, 'Outspoken and Often Ironic Essays on Personally Selected Points of English Style on Which the Author's Opinions Often Happily Correspond to Those of Many Other Good and Careful Writers'. Such informative explicitness has become rare on title-pages since the 17th century, but what Ben Jonson and James Greenwood found useful might well be reintroduced by writers on subjects such as usage, where *quot homines tot sententiae*. At any rate, this particular putative subtitle continues to be suitable for the new Fowler, thanks to the wisdom in selecting for the revision an editor as widely read as Gowers, as humane of interest, as effective in what our cousins call 'communication skills', and as sympathetic to the great institution entrusted to him.

Being something of an 'instinctive grammatical moralizer' himself, Sir Ernest preserves Fowler's special interest in cultivating an unmannered, unpedantic, unpompous, inoffensive style. As a general principle in his own independent writings on English, he insists on unmuffling the woollinesses to which most of us are prone when we try to write seriously; he insists on cleaning up the sloppinesses we indulge in when we try to write too much too fast. In refurbishing *Modern English Usage*, he keeps Fowler's arguments, witticisms, and opinions whenever in conscience he possibly can, discreetly replacing rather passé examples with more topical ones from what must be an extraordinarily rich collection of illiterate, semi-literate, and (most relished of all, no doubt) hyper-literate quotations. At times, he keeps Fowler's prejudices too: the article on 'Literary Critics' Words' (which some critics have hopefully felt was at least out of date) retains all its old acerbity and is even somewhat extended.

He also keeps, as the last point suggests, most of the esoteric headings that fit only bizarrely in an alphabetical reference-book: 'Battered Ornaments', 'Cannibalism', 'False Scent', 'Hanging-Up', 'Legerdemain', 'Object-Shuffling', 'Out of the Frying-Pan',

'Swapping Horses', 'Unequal Yoke-Fellows'. Dull family gatherings have been enlivened for two generations by 'Fowler Bees', where the object is to guess what such entries are about ('Cannibalism?—Oh yes, that must be on prepositions'). On the other hand, Sir Ernest is more in the spirit of the 1960s in being considerably less dogmatic, often toning down the impatience of the earlier entry; in being more tolerant not of pomposity but of the more venial sin of colloquialism; in being sensibly disinclined to kick against the pricks of established usage, however 'monstrous'; and above all in being more sensitive than Fowler was to the reasonable needs of usage to vary according to a user's particular purpose on a particular occasion.

The Gowers-Fowler is an admirable piece of work which will entertain and educate all who browse in it. But it still leaves the field wide open for someone to supply us with a book on Modern English Usage—a book that would tell us about the stringing-together of English words as easily, objectively, authoritatively, and completely as any good dictionary already tells us about the words themselves in (relative) isolation. The desiderata are coverage, judgment, and organization. Coverage involves a major investigation and observation of spoken and written English, analogous to the long-term lexical observation that underlies the great *Oxford English Dictionary* from which the distinguished range of small, 'practical' Oxford dictionaries has been derived. Judgment involves linguistic and psycholinguistic research into the relative acceptability of the immense variety of English phrase and sentence structures, with particular reference to the medium and occasion influencing acceptability. Organization involves devising a way of presenting the data and recommendations so that these are accessible for easy reference. Unlike the 'words' which are a dictionary's business, the abstractions relating to grammar, usage, idiom, and style do not—as we have seen—easily lend themselves to alphabetic treatment ('Cannibalism' really is about prepositions, among other things).

All this is a tall order ('Hackneyed Phrases'). If the order were not so tall ('Novelty Hunting'), we would not still need to order it ('Legerdemain'). Meantime, we have Gowers-Fowler ('Sobriquet') and it is likely to be a long time before this fascinating, wise, urbane, information-filled volume ('Hyperbole') will be superseded ('Spelling Points').

NOTES

1. Broadcast in March 1958.
2. This review of Sir Ernest Gowers' revision of Fowler (Clarendon Press, 1965) appeared in a shorter version in the *New Statesman*, 21 November 1965.

10 Speech and Communication

Occasionally someone draws our attention afresh to the fact that of all the forms that English takes today in its regional and social distribution, and of all the forms that it has taken in the past, the one that calls out most pressingly for attention, for research into its grammatical structure, is the living spoken English of educated people. This is no trifling side-issue needing the pleas of an enthusiast: yet it continues to elude attention down to the present time, except for the welcome appearance of some studies in recent years, largely undertaken with a strictly pedagogical aim, by colleagues concerned with 'English as a Foreign Language'. It is almost incredible that after some three hundred years of active and continuous academic interest in the English language, we should still be without an even moderately detailed description of the English we speak, as opposed to the English we write.

Of course, we have long been aware of some rather vague distinctions. In our own time, and in previous generations too, grammarians have offered us comments, value judgments, on the difference between spoken and written English—almost always to the detriment of the former, and generally couched in terms borrowed from activities and disciplines other than grammar. They have called spoken English *less polished* than written English, using a lapidary's term; or, they have called it *looser*, perhaps drawing the image from the chandler's bundles of firewood. Or they have called it less *logical*. William Cobbett the Radical, for example, often raised this particular objection. He hated any illogical qualification of words which ought in his view to be considered as absolutes—particularly the word *reform*, say, which to Cobbett was most sacredly absolute: you either reformed something, or you did not reform it. On one occasion he took a Whig MP severely to task for the muddleheadedness of professing to be in favour of '*moderate* reform'. How, asked Cobbett, would the

---

An earlier form of this paper was published in *Studies in Communication*, ed. Ifor Evans (London 1955).

same gentleman 'like to obtain *moderate justice* in a court of law, or to meet with *moderate chastity* in a wife?' (Letter 18 of *A Grammar of the English Language*, London 1833).

But apart from such ex cathedra statements about the quality of colloquial 'looseness', grammarians of earlier generations concentrated their attention almost exclusively on written English. Even in our own time it has been fashionable to think of speech as being different from the real stuff of language (as represented in neat printed sentences) only in peripheral and trivial ways.

In this paper, I wish to present for discussion two kinds of material: see passages I and II, pp. 107–8. The first is a brief sample of Bulwer Lytton's partly facetious, partly satirical, yet presumably realistic attempt to demonstrate some features which seemed to him characteristic of the speech of his educated contemporaries, in the decade or so before the Victorian era began. (*England and the English*, 1833, I. 156 ff). The second selection of material comprises simplified transcriptions made of random conversations, recorded electronically and—be it said—secretly: so that the speakers should not be made nervous or be otherwise influenced by the presence of a microphone into falsifying their natural speech structure. The speakers are university graduates: graduates in English. I emphasize this in case there is doubt about the standard of education (or indeed intelligence) attained by the informants. There need in fact be no fear that the present age has totally departed from such aims and principles of education as Ascham laid down in 1570, when he said, of teaching children: 'I wishe to have them speake so, as it may well appeare, that the braine doth governe the tongue, and that reason leadeth forth the taulke' (*The Scholemaster*, p. 29). Rather, if the untidiness and apparent confusion are rather startling, it is because we are unaccustomed to seeing the actual events of speech in written form. Indeed, our reading habits tend to persuade us that the dialogue of contemporary plays, and the pieces within quotation marks in novels, are precisely what speech is actually like: we forget that such dialogue is synthetic, and is *written* before it is spoken or read. It is an imaginative attempt by a *writer* to represent speech, and even a writer like Pinter with a talent for capturing colloquial structures cannot forget that the primary function of the dialogue is to be the vehicle for his plot.

It is a commonplace that most people are surprised and often ashamed when they hear their voices on a recording for the first time. But that is nothing to what their feelings would be if they were shown a transcript of their everyday chatter. No-one likes to believe that he stammers and splutters in fits and starts, but for the most part he probably does nevertheless. Of course, the flow of speech is fairly steady so long as we are merely passing the time of day, with stereotyped greetings, or comments on the weather. These things come out smoothly and usually without hesitation because they are conventional reflexes, acts of behaviour almost as automatic as blinking when a speck of dust gets in one's eye. But the more intelligent and genuinely communicative the conversation we are trying to hold, the more absurd our words would look on paper if all we said were taken down verbatim.

By the same token, if we could now *hear* these samples which we are in fact able only to *read*, there would be little impression of oddity: they would not seem incoherent, nor unduly marred with splutters and anacolutha. In 1779, Fanny Burney made an attempt to show on paper just how ridiculously a certain man talked, and having done so, she adds this significant comment: 'I think . . . his language looks more absurd upon paper even than it sounds in conversation' (*Madame D'Arblay*, I. 256). Bulwer Lytton is also at pains to insist that the material used in this present paper is *by no means caricatured*: the speaker, he says, is even 'reckoned a very sensible man' and listeners find 'nothing inconclusive in the elucidation' (op. cit., I.133). This may seem clearer if the reader makes the attempt of realizing the speech orally, 'acting' it aloud, and then tries to do the same for the non-fictitious and contemporary material.

To the extent that the genuine recorded conversation seems fantastic and impossible only as a piece of writing, this is because the eye and the ear are not used to sharing—indeed are not in many cases capable of assimilating—the same linguistic material, any more than the tongue and pen are capable of reproducing the same linguistic material. An extreme example is the English of legal documents, where a glance at a fire insurance policy will remind one that English of this kind would be unintelligible if heard instead of read; in the same way, no ordinary person—however educated—can speak this kind of English, he can only write it. As T. S. Eliot puts it,

> People sometimes talk vaguely about the *conversational style* in writing. Still more often, they deplore the divorce between the language as spoken and the language as written. It is true that the spoken and the written language can drift too far apart – with the eventual consequence of forming a new written language. But what is overlooked is that an *identical* spoken and written language would be practically intolerable. If we spoke as we write we should find no one to listen: and if we wrote as we speak we should find no one to read. The spoken and written language must not be too near together, as they must not be too far apart.
>
> 'Charles Wibley', in *Selected Essays* (London, 1949), p. 459.

The usefulness to the grammarian—to the linguist—of studying transcribed speech should be obvious. Only in speech can we find the unpremeditated, the natural phenomena of English; only when we have arrested speech and have it in some form of cold storage, can it become material for the analyst; it ceases then to have but a momentary existence, making but a fleeting and often misleading impression upon even the most watchful student: it can then be studied, pondered over.

For our present purpose, it will suffice to use an orthographic transcription but it is important to realize that a good deal of the special features that Eliot has in mind as characterizing spoken language are endemic in the sound pattern and can be rendered only by means of a *prosodic* transcription. There are examples in Ch. 12. No attempt has been made to divide up the transcription into units by means of the battery of conventional punctuation marks. The reader may like to try for himself, but the position is that in the last resort speech is not susceptible to the divisions indicated by conventional punctuation and—equally—the prosodic units that would be distinguished in a fuller transcription defy registration in terms of graphic punctuation.

What is true for prosodic distinctions is to a considerable extent true for grammatical distinctions as well: there is often a lack of one-for-one correspondence between the features of spoken and written language. The implications of this are important in considering the oral transmission of written materials. Through the medium of radio and public address systems, a great deal of information is delivered orally from written sources: or, to put it the other way round, we are constantly being expected to listen and react to spoken information and directives, which were fashioned in terms of another medium, the visual phenomenon of written English. But the criteria for a 'good' sentence on paper do not necessarily match, one might suggest, those for a 'good' sentence in oral transmission: after all, as we have just seen, there are numerous aspects of natural, spoken English that have no direct correspondence with the features of a sentence on paper. This is something to which we shall return in a short time, since it is likely to have an interesting bearing upon our ability to comprehend written materials when we hear them read to us instead of reading them ourselves:—with our difficulty, for example, in following a lecture which is read out in entirety, instead of being delivered from notes, or, better still, without notes.

Let us now consider a passage from a seventeenth-century book on the art of speaking, associated with that cultivated body, the Gentlemen of the Port Royal:

'Tis an effect of the Wisdom of God, who created Man to be happy, that whatever is useful to his conversation [by which is meant something like 'his way of life'] is agreeable to him. The pleasure annex'd to all the actions that can preserve his life, carries him freely and spontaneously to them. We find it no pain to eat, because the gust and relish of the Meat discovers the necessity of eating to be agreeable: And that which authoriseth this Observation, that God has joined the usefulness and pleasure together is this, because all Victual that conduces to nourishment is relishable, whereas other things that cannot be assimulated and be turn'd into our substance, are insipid.

This seasoning of Necessity with Delight, is to be found in the Use of speech. There is a strange sympathy betwixt the Voice of those who speak, and the Ears of those who hear: Words that are spoken with pain, are offensive to the Hearer . . . A Discourse cannot be pleasant to the Hearer, that is not easie to the Speaker; nor can it be easily pronounc'd, unless it be heard with delight.

We feed with more appetite upon wholsom and relishable Meats: we listen more easily to a Discourse, whose smoothness lessens the trouble of attending. It is with Sciences as with Meats: We must endeavour to make those things pleasant, that are useful . . . [T]he Ease of the Speaker, causes the satisfaction of the Hearer. Let us then endeavour . . . to discover what is to be avoided in the ranging of our Words . . .

> The Art of Speaking (London, 1696), pp. 123–5; from the French of Bernard Lamy.

We need not lend our entire support to the food analogy, or to the writer's views on what the cyberneticists like to call homœostasis: they are certainly somewhat at variance in spirit with Langland's teaching that 'all is not good to the ghost that the gut asketh'. But it may be of interest to follow up the idea suggested about speech. I would wish, in this connection, to comment on just two features of spoken English which seem to be worth picking on because they are of frequent occurrence and have some bearing on what we have been saying.

In the first line of passage II we find the sequence: 'I've been very interested in the Elizabethan dialogue—how to read it without being too amused by it', where the same informant would doubtless have *written*: 'I've been interested in how to read the Elizabethan dialogue without being too amused by it'. The prepositional phrase in the latter (*in* + clause) appears in the former as a quasi-appositive structure (*in* + {noun phrase ≡ clause}). This is superficially illogical. The Elizabethan dialogue is not the same as 'how to read it'; moreover, the speaker is not really saying that he is interested in the Elizabethan dialogue but rather in *how to read* the Elizabethan dialogue. In any case, the 'apposition' is impossible since the noun phrase *the Elizabethan dialogue* outside the clause is in a genuinely appositive relation to a pronoun, *it*, within the clause.

Nevertheless, the illogical sequence that occurs in the transcription is strictly analogous to a disjunctive construction which extends far back in English linguistic history and seems to be a genuine feature of colloquial style. In the *Anchoresses' Rule*, a book written some seven hundred and fifty years ago, we find: 'pe wrecche poure peoddere mare nurð he makeð to ȝeien his sape pen pe riche mercer al his deorewurðe ware'—'The poor miserable peddlar, more noise he makes to cry his soap, than a rich merchant all his costly goods' (as edited by J. R. R. Tolkien, EETS.OS 249, 1962, p. 36). Here too a noun phrase, *The poor miserable peddlar*, is appositive to a pronoun, *he*, in the clause that follows.

The type of structure illustrated by 'I'm interested in the Elizabethan dialogue—how to read it' is a constantly recurring one among the spontaneous recordings of modern English that we have made and its frequency is rather striking also in attempts made in literature (notably in dramatic dialogue) to represent natural spoken English. It seems reasonable to suppose that it comes *easier* to a speaker to disjoin an important noun phrase in this way than to incorporate it immediately into the clause in which it has its proper grammatical relation. Unfortunate perhaps, from an aesthetic viewpoint, but apparently true. We appear then to have the Port Royal 'ease of the speaker': is such ease in fact correlated with the satisfaction of the hearer? In other terms, we appear to have a structure that is suited to the human encoding system: is there any evidence that it lends itself particularly readily to the human decoding process as well?

An attempt was made to investigate the possibility experimentally. The first step was to construct a message whose complexity would practically ensure that no one would manage to take it in when presented orally so as to be able to reproduce it in entirety. The next step was to arrange the message in the alternative patterns we have been discussing, with and without appositive disjunction. The alternative forms were as follows:

A. He's doing research on the mineral resources of various parts of the Commonwealth—the procedures for assessing, the methods of surveying and the techniques for exploiting them.

B. He's doing research on the procedures for assessing, the methods of surveying and the techniques for exploiting the mineral resources of various parts of the Commonwealth.

Both provide exactly the same 'information', and for scoring purposes this information was regarded as comprising ten equal units: seven content units ('research', 'mineral', 'resources', 'Commonwealth', 'assessing', 'surveying', 'exploiting') and three units of significant arrangement: research on (mineral) resources; resources of (parts of) Commonwealth; exploitation the final goal. Apart from the fact that the first version contains one more word than the second (the weakly stressed appositive *them* at the end), the two forms differ only in the *arrangement* of words. They were tested out on two groups of undergraduates in the English Department of University College London. Each group comprised about 35 first and second year students, in roughly equal proportions, and no information on the reason for the experiment was given to either group. The two versions of the test-piece occupied the same reading time, and the rate of reading was very fast, as a final check against one hundred per cent perception and recall which would of course have yielded data that were worthless for comparison. The group that were given A, the more colloquial version, absorbed on average sixty per cent of the information, as measured by their ability to recall or paraphrase. The group that were given B, the 'literary' version, on average absorbed only forty-five per cent. Thus, with even this brief text, one group of informants understood *three-twentieths* more of the information, when a normal literary English version was modified in the direction of a style that we have seen to be natural in unprepared speech. This seems to bear out the Port Royal suggestion that 'There is a strange sympathy betwixt the Voice of those who speak, and the Ears of those who hear . . . A Discourse cannot be pleasant to the Hearer that is not easie to the Speaker . . . '

The colloquial device we have been discussing involves disjuncture with the effect of *foregrounding* a lexical cluster of special importance in the communication.[1]

The second feature of speech to which I should like to draw attention also involves disjuncture, but this time with a downgrading or parenthesis of the structure disjoined. I refer to the interlarding of our everyday talk with a small number of frequently recurring low-stressed items such as *you know*, *you see*, and *well*. It is easily demonstrable that these play no part grammatically in the transmission of information: they can be omitted leaving sentences which are both grammatically whole and synonymous. Yet not only is speech constantly embellished with them at the present time, but popular talk stretching back to Shakespeare and beyond has been similarly peppered with these well-nigh meaningless items. With the Bulwer Lytton examples in lines 3, 8, 13 etc, we may compare the less obtrusive (since not burlesque) examples in the passage of natural speech: lines 14, 17 etc.

Now, I have just called these items 'well-nigh meaningless', but that does not mean that they are well-nigh functionless. In a separate test that I carried out on the two groups of students already mentioned, I asked them to comment on the differences between two forms of utterance carrying the same 'information' and differing only in the presence or absence of a parenthetical *you know* and *you see*. As one would expect from students with a professional interest in literary style, the majority deplored the more prolix form on these grounds; at the same time, they indicated in their commentary that they nevertheless regarded the more verbose form as *friendlier, more informal*, and so possessed of qualities which might render this form preferable if one's standards of judgment were other than aesthetic.

It appears in fact that *you know* and *you see* and similar items might be called 'intimacy signals'—trifling signals emitted disjunctively, apart from the main grammatical complex,[2] which have as their aim the cultivation of intimacy between the speaker and the hearer, items which draw the hearer to the speaker, make him feel at ease, and help prevent obstacles from impairing the easy flow of stimulus and response. And obviously, since the desire to feel that the hearer is *sharing* something with us seems to be fundamental in our urge to speak,[3] these sharing devices, these intimacy signals in our everyday talk, are of considerable importance. Unlike the structural contrast that we discussed a page or so earlier, the present contrast—the presence or absence of intimacy signals—appears to have little or no influence upon the amount of information the hearer absorbs, though more protracted and detailed tests may reveal their influence also in this direction. But they certainly seem to have a marked influence upon the hearer's emotional attitude and reaction to the *speaker*, and therefore—indirectly—to what he is saying. At a time when more and more is being heard about the necessity for cultivating good relations between various groups and individuals in the growing complexity of our society, it is obviously highly relevant to devote some study to devices that appear to have social and emotive significance. It may well be that when some people strike their fellows as cool, abrupt, dogmatic, unsympathetic, or who otherwise stimulate an undesirable resistance, even hostility, the cause may lie in the difference between actual and expected speech forms such as these intimacy signals. To quote the Port Royal book again, 'We must endeavour to make those things pleasant, that are useful'.

These two features on which I have been making preliminary and inadequate observations are in a sense perhaps but two aspects of the same phenomenon, one that has long been recognized as characterizing spoken English—and much criticized as such: namely, redundancy. Both features involve speakers to a greater or lesser extent in a prolixity which is avoided by the neater structures used in written English where the special conditions of reading allow us to compensate for brevity on the one hand or complexity on the other. And both in Bulwer Lytton's 'Impressions' and in my own transcriptions it will be seen that there is much further evidence of redundancy, notably in the repetition of words or parts of words. Much of this redundancy must strike us as lamentable and absurd (especially when we read it rather than hear it), and much no doubt could and ought to be eradicated by means of the various methods of training people to find fitter and readier expression for their thoughts. But we should not be unduly disparaging towards the redundancies of colloquial speech.

A similar situation may still obtain, but certainly in the conditions of war-time signalling, when meteorological information was teleprinted to air stations, economically and efficiently encoded, it was strictly required that the two most vital items of information so far as air safety was concerned were repeated in a different form. In other words, redundancy was deliberately introduced so that receivers could have a chance of checking the accuracy of the information. A more commonplace analogy is presented by our habit of spelling out numbers on telegrams, increasing the cost of transmission but decreasing the possibility of error, since the spelled-out forms have redundancy where arabic symbols have not. If such deliberate redundancy is necessary to the successful use of these channels of communication, there may be more justification than we sometimes feel in the redundancies of everyday spoken English.

To sum up, then, I am suggesting that some of the relatively untidy and often deplored features of everyday speech appear to play a rather important role in two aspects of the communication act: the efficient transmission of information on the one hand, and on the other, the establishment of a relationship fostering willingness to receive. Some colloquial patterns appear to be both more readily encoded and more readily decoded than the alternative and synonymous ones which bear the stamp of literary approval. Many colloquial forms and patterns have not yet been consciously apprehended or submitted to a linguist's analysis for their linguistic or cultural significance to be investigated. Some of the most glaringly prolix items of speech, like *you know* and *you see*, seem to have a function, in conditioning the reception given to what we are saying. By all means let us be concerned to 'improve our English' but let us at the same time have more work done on spoken language so that we do not find ourselves encouraging people to tidy out of existence some of the litter that society finds pleasant and useful, some of the ease and pleasantness which, in the Port Royal book's terms, is 'heard with delight'. The matter is put in a more extreme form in *The Brothers Karamazov* (Book 6, Ch. 3): 'If the people around you are spiteful and callous, and will not hear you, fall down before them and beg their forgiveness; for in truth you are to blame for their not wanting to hear you.'

I *Bulwer Lytton's Impressions of English Speech, c.* 1830

'No—I assure you—now er—er—that—er—it was the most shocking accident possible—er—poor Chester was riding in the Park—er—you know that grey —er (substantive dropped, hand a little flourished instead)—of his—splendid creature!—well sir, and by Jove—er—the—er (no substantive, flourish again)—took fright, and—e—er—' here the gentleman throws up his chin and eyes, sinks back exhausted into his chair, and after a pause adds, 'Well, they took him into—the shop—there—you know—with the mahogany sashes—just by the Park—er—and the—er—man there—set his—what d'ye call it—er—collar-bone; but he was——er—ter-ri-bly—terribly'—a full stop. The gentleman shakes his head—and the sentence is suspended to eternity.

'Oh, I can tell you exactly—ehem—he said you see, that he disliked the ministers, and so forth you understand—but that—er—in these times, and so forth—and with this river of blood—oh! he was very fine *there!*—you must read it—well, sir; and then he was very good against O'Connell, capital—and all this agitation going on—and murder, and so forth—and then, sir, he told a capital story, about a man and his wife being murdered, and putting a child in the fireplace—you see—I forget now, but it was capital; and then he wound up with—a—with—a—in his usual way, in short. Oh! he quite justified himself—you understand . . .'

II *Transcriptions of Natural Speech, c.* 1950

(–, – –, – – – indicate relative lengths of pause)

I've been very interested in – – the Elizabethan dialogue – how how to read it without – – – being too amused by it and the the irony the – sarcasm a particular point is – in the Malcontent when this Malevole – he's supposed to be party to a plot to kill Ferneze – Ferneze is killed – – supposedly – and is on the floor – supposedly dead – and he starts groaning and – Malevole shouts – what more proclamations – what news from Limbo – – and I've tried to think – to find out what attitude of mind this is – – that can – do things like that.

He – seemed of course he had that kind of n er I I'm er I I er I I er er are you northern by any chance I was going to say that kind of northern – – er – scepticism or at least questioning mind – – which er – but of course he would mislead you with that he er he gave you the impression that he only er you know he gave you the impression that he was – sceptical and at times sceptical and nothing else – – – but I think he er – – I think he appreciated the course there you know – from one or two things he said when I bumped into him

All the time he tries to maintain a balance he talks about naturalism in education and and – he's started on pragmatism – I haven't had time to follow up this in in my reading at all but – all the time – he tries – – er to maintain a balance I mean he he he criticizes points of the naturalistic approach of the – approach of of of er the er er um originating from Rousseau – and then he criticizes um points in the pragmatic approach – test of experience all the time he criticizes that he says it doesn't allow enough weight – for – the value er of tradition – all the time he tries to maintain this balance – but – curiously enough this week there – is a report of a a a talk of his there's a talk – – um er er a lecture or whatever you like to call it er er a talk given by him – in which – which is rather helpful because it does make his – point of view I think er his points of view a little clearer you know it it wasn't of such a negative quality as his er as his lectures you see which have to maintain this more neutral quality shall I say which have to maintain this balance all the time you see

NOTES

1. On 'foregrounding', see R. Quirk and A. H. Smith, *The Teaching of English* (London, 1959), pp. 44 f, and G. N. Leech, *A Linguistic Guide to English Poetry* (London, 1969), pp. 56 ff.

2. *You know* and *you see* may alternatively of course be part of a grammatical complex, in which they do not function as 'intimacy signals'; formal criteria can readily be found to distinguish between the function of *you know* in 'You know (that) I can't do it' and 'You know, I can't do it'.

3. Cf. B. Malinowski, 'The Problem of Meaning in Primitive Languages', in C. K. Ogden and I. A. Richards, *The Meaning of Meaning* (8th edition, London, 1946), pp. 313–316.

11 Linguistics, Usage, and the User

In approaching linguistics, we may have any of several questions in our minds. What is the nature of human language? How is the study of linguistics, the scientific study of human language, actually organized? What bearing do language and linguistics have upon our understanding of other areas of inquiry? I would like to pursue yet another line and ask what bearing linguistics has on language—on our language, English, and on us as users of English.

Linguistics has provided us with our dictionaries and grammars of English. But this rather bald and deceptively self-evident statement requires careful scrutiny. It does not mean, for example, that the dictionaries and grammars of English in common use have been designed by linguists: it means that the compilers of dictionaries and grammars have been informed by some linguistic theory or other, because they could not otherwise have even made a start on such work. But so venerable is the tradition of lexicography and grammar-writing that very few of those carrying out such work have felt the need to engage in the issues that have been especially exciting linguists of the past twenty years. It is necessary to insist on this because it is sometimes alleged that, because dictionaries by Onions, Barnhart, Gove or grammars by Curme, Long, Zandvoort seem to reflect so little of what is currently dominant in linguistics, they reflect no linguistics at all. They do, of course. The work of such men rests confidently, if not exactly securely, on the accumulated wisdom of linguistic scholarship stretching back over centuries, on the whole retaining what has been found permanent and true, skimming off what has been suspected to be merely fashionable and false. This is why English grammars and dictionaries of 1870 do not strike us as wildly different in approach, format or content from grammars and dictionaries of 1970, whereas if we take Chomsky's *Aspects* of 1965 and

---

This paper was presented as the concluding lecture (February 1970) in a series organized by the Institute of ContemporaryArts and published in *Linguistics at Large*, ed. N. Minnis (London, 1971).

W. D. Whitneys' *Language and the Study of Language* of 1867, we appear to have two separate disciplines with widely differing frames of reference.

But my statement that linguistics has given us dictionaries and grammars requires further scrutiny. It implies—correctly and very importantly—that linguistics supplies us with standards by which we can speak of one dictionary or grammar as being better in some respect than another. We need to be careful, however, about the use of 'better' here. For reasons that are by no means fully understood, there is a widespread, deep seated and apparently well-nigh ineradicable belief that good usage comes to us from dictionaries and grammars; and that it is the task of these works not merely to identify the rules of good lexical or grammatical use but to determine them—perhaps even, in some sense, create them. On this basis, a grammar or dictionary may be adjudged less good than another according as the author has described the rules for a usage of which the critic disapproves, much as one Anglican bishop might be adjudged less good than another if he had added a tenet from Buddhism to the thirty-nine articles.

Let me illustrate the two ways in which 'not good' could be applied to a single rule. If a grammarian said that all English verbs were made negative by the introduction of the auxiliary *do* followed by *not* and the infinitive, as in *He drank—He did not drink*, a linguist might criticize the rule because it would permit the ungrammatical *He did not be cold* as the negative of *He was cold*. No such objection would cross a lay critic's mind, but he might on the other hand object that the grammarian's rule would permit *He used to go* to be negated as *He didn't use to go*, and this, he may say, is 'bad grammar'.

Similarly, a linguist may criticize a dictionary entry because a word is poorly defined or given an incorrect etymology. A lay critic may object to a definition because a meaning is given of which he disapproves (*terrific* with the sense 'splendid', for example); and he will object to the appearance of some entries altogether: many Americans protested at Gove's including *ain't* in the 1961 *Webster*, and there are plenty of four-letter words which the British too would want to exclude, even in our present permissive phase.

It is easy to see the two senses of 'good' and to confer a superior smile on the layman's use of it. This is not to say, however, that the lay use can be dismissed as involving an attitude that is irrelevant, or a sociolinguistic problem for which we already have the solution. The attitude is so far from being irrelevant as to underlie a large part of the layman's purpose in interesting himself—even to the small extent that he does—in dictionaries and grammars at all. And the lexicographer's and grammarian's problem lies to no small extent in trying to satisfy the perfectly legitimate needs and interests of the lay user. He must ask himself which or how many of the varieties of English he is going to take into account in his grammar or dictionary; how he is going to categorize them and their interrelations; how—even more fundamentally—he is going to acquire the data on these varieties. Though the native grammarian or lexicographer has in one sense complete knowledge of the language he is describing and this can be used as an invaluable gauge to check data and test rules, he knows that variation among individuals can be very considerable and that he must make sure that it is the community's language he is describing and not his own idiolect. Moreover, it is no easy task to pour out all the knowledge even of one's own language, let alone do so in a systematic, well-ordered, and of course objective manner. Both on theoretical and on practical grounds, therefore, grammarians and lexicographers have had to devise ways of observing other people's usage, paying careful attention to objectivity and to principles of selection.

The Survey of English Usage at University College London is concerned with scrutinizing and describing the *grammar* rather than the *lexicon* of present-day educated English, but the categorization of sources in Fig. 1 is applicable to both fields. Broadly speaking, all present-day dictionaries of English place ultimate reliance solely on a *printed corpus*. This is of course a great advance over the days when items were included on a haphazard basis and when definitions were promoted primarily by the lexicographer's own opinion of the correct meaning. Modern practice still leaves a good deal to be desired, however. For example, it has been possible now for a quarter of a century to collect a corpus of spoken English fairly easily and inexpensively through the advent of the tape recorder. Every lexicographer knows that most new words and most new meanings of existing words are current in speech before they appear in print—and that it is a matter of chance not merely *when* but *whether* they get into print. One respects the lexicographer's reasons for clinging to printed sources (notably, their public verifiability) but it is high time that methods were evolved to admit this primary type of source material. Secondly, little or nothing has been done in lexicography to develop scientific techniques for supplementing corpus (in which the occurrence of 'self-defining' quotations is necessarily fortuitous) by elicitation techniques in order to attain a fuller record of the words we know and the meanings we assign them. One obvious reason for this is that a corpus can give us only positive information: that a word exists and exists in a certain sense; it cannot give us the negative information that a word or meaning has ceased to exist. As a result, it is extremely difficult for dictionaries to be other than out of date since in revising an earlier edition

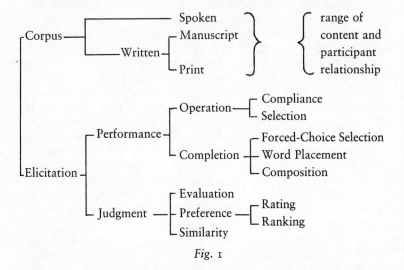

Fig. 1

the lexicographer has not the means of proving that his predecessors' work is invalid in any respect except incompleteness. For example, the latest *Concise Oxford* (1964), in most respects an excellent revision, gives as its entire and sole definition of *terrific*, 'Causing terror, terrible'.

Another reason for needing elicitation techniques is that definition solely by scrutiny of corpus-derived quotation, while admirable in inhibiting the lexicographer's imagination and personal prejudice, is almost inevitably prevented from achieving the full semantic subtlety that characterizes verbal usage. For example, for all its 2000 handsome pages, the new *Random House Dictionary* (1966) is not alone in equating the adverb *utterly* with *completely*. But we have found that, in artificial supplementation of corpus by completion tests (where subjects were asked to complete sentences where a beginning was supplied like 'The man utterly – – – – –')[1], the adverb was freely used to intensify verbs like *hate, disagree, detest, despise* but we were not offered verbs like *love, mend, restore*. The point is clinched by an elicitation technique that we call 'forced-choice selection' testing. Given

I – – – – – detest her
I – – – – – agree with you
(completely, utterly)

where we require the two blanks to be filled from the alternatives (each of which can be used once only), subjects predominantly put *utterly* into the blank before *detest*, where of course if it really was equivalent to *completely* there would be a random distribution of the two adverbs.

Again, we will not easily find a dictionary that explains the reason for our unhesitating choice between *munch* and *chew* in this pair of sentences:

> He – – – – – the bacon
> He – – – – – the bacon reluctantly
> (chewed, munched)

and indeed we will be lucky if our dictionary attempts to make any distinction at all between the two verbs. The *Concise Oxford* defines *scuttle* solely in terms of hurrying from danger; it even uses the verb 'fly' as a gloss in this connection. If this were the whole truth recognized by even the least sensitive native user of English, *scuttle* would fit either of the following blanks with equal satisfaction for him:

> The mouse – – – – – towards the door
> The mouse – – – – – silently towards the door
> (darted, scuttled)

But it is very unlikely that many of us would agree to a random use of the two verbs here.

In short, and without going into other aspects of contemporary dictionaries that could be improved in the light of recent linguistic research, we may look for a great deal of change in lexicographical method during the next generation which will result in dictionaries reacting to usage much more sensitively than they do at present, and without sacrificing the admirable standards of objectivity they have developed.

The problems in compiling a grammar are much greater than in compiling a dictionary, since the objects to be described (sentences, clauses, phrases, modal usages etc) are much more abstract and less discrete. There are, it is true, some respects in which the grammarian's task seems easier: his field of study seems to be more limited and more stable than that of the lexicographer. No one knows all the words even in the *Concise Oxford* and not even the most widely read lexicographer can have a week go by without coming upon a new word in his daily paper. By contrast, we rarely have the impression that we are reading or hearing a new grammatical structure.

Even so, the grammarian's problem in assembling the data for his description is not dissimilar from the lexicographer's, and we may refer back to Fig. 1. Again, we have the need for a corpus of other people's usage as our basis: the risk of bias, idiosyncracy or sheer uncertainty is even greater with a grammarian's introspection than with a lexicographer's. How do we decide when to say 'I gave the girl a book' and when to say 'I gave a book to the girl'? How do we decide whether we normally say 'I didn't dare to answer', 'I didn't dare answer' or 'I dared not answer'?

As for extending the corpus beyond the traditional type of printed material, the Survey of English Usage considers that for grammatical research it is essential to have adequate samples of unprepared speech and free conversation and also to collect written material in manuscript form as well as in print. There is no reason to doubt that our organization of sentences is very different as between speaking and even the most casual letter, irrespective of whatever difference there may or may not be in our use of vocabulary. We know that a perhaps even greater change comes over our sentence structure when we are preparing a more formal piece of writing—even some announcement for a notice board. Finally, anyone who has had a piece of work published knows that house style makes numerous changes necessary before a manuscript goes into print.

But essential as a carefully planned and representative corpus is, we are still left with the obvious deficiencies that are inherent in any corpus: it is inevitably an incomplete inventory of the possible grammatical patterns in a language, and quotations are in any case too often inadequate to enable us to specify the precise rules governing their structure. We therefore pay close attention to the need for acquiring information by means of elicitation techniques. Most of our work in this area has been with *compliance* tests, in which subjects hear (not see) a sentence and are told to carry out some small change and then to write down the sentence otherwise unaltered. For example, they might be given the sentence 'He probably will buy a car' and be told to replace *He* by *She*. The interest to us would be of course the number of subjects who—despite the instructions—would write down *She will probably buy a car*, having moved the adverb from in front of the auxiliary verb, thus giving us unsolicited a clear indication of their preference in the matter. But since I used forced-choice selection tests to illustrate elicitation for lexical information, let me use this type[2] also to show how grammatical information can be elicited.

If we were asked what difference there was between *I watched her dance* and *I watched her dancing*, we would be quite likely to say that there is very little. This certainly has been the view of most authors of English grammars. But if we were given the following and asked to fill the blanks with *dance* or *dancing*:

I watched her – – – – – for hours
I watched her – – – – – on one occasion

we would probably associate *dancing* with the former and *dance*
with the latter, thus indicating that we recognize an aspectual
difference. Similarly, although we have all known that the verb *to
wet* had two alternative forms of past tense ('He wet it', 'He
wetted it'), it has not been generally known, until the Survey's
tests demonstrated it, that there is a semantic distinction between
them in that they will not be randomly distributed by a forced
choice in the two sentences:

The artist – – – – – the paper carefully
The baby – – – – – the bed last night

Yet another reason for needing elicitation technique is that we
need to know not merely the facts of usage but also the attitudes
to particular usages. It is still not sufficiently realized that
between the universally acknowledged well-formed structures and
the opposite pole of structures whose ill-formedness is acknowledged equally universally there is a large mass of usage where
opinion is divided.

But it is still less clearly realized that both our usage and our
attitudes to usage are conditioned by several sharply different
factors and that the relation between acceptability and usage is
complex and indirect. Fig. 2 attempts to display some of the chief
variables.[3] It will be noticed that, within the material derived
from elicitation techniques, we need a distinction between 'habitual' and 'potential' usage. In particular, it is often useful to distinguish those features of an elicited sentence which an informant
can be presumed to have commonly experienced: the past of
learn or the placing of *hardly* between auxiliary and main verb,
for example. These could be regarded as 'habitual'. By contrast,
elicitation might seek the use of an item that the informant may
never have experienced but which is nevertheless in some sense
'available' to him. For example, he might have to supply a past for
a strange new verb like /flaiv/ or show where he would place the
adverb *introductorily* in a sentence. Not all instances of 'potential'
use are as clear as these, but when it is considered how invariant
or 'idiomatic' usage can be at the opposite pole (for example 'Far
be it from me' which does not allow us to form *'Near be this to
her') one realizes the significance of rules that are to be derived
from 'potential' rather than relatively 'habitual' use.

The diagram goes on to state that use may be conditioned or
unconditioned. Such conditioning may be situational (as when a
formal occasion prompts a formal usage) or it may be linguistic.

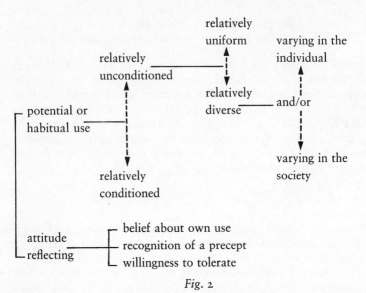

Fig. 2

For example, although one can generally permute the preposi-tional phrases in the structure *talk to* N₁ *about* N₂ there is a lin-guistic condition forbidding this when N₁ and N₂ are co-referen-tial. Thus

> I talked to Harry about the play
> I talked about the play to Harry
> I talked to Harry about himself

but not   *I talked about himself to Harry
or   *I talked about Harry to himself

Where an item is towards the relatively unconditioned end of the graded scale, use may be relatively uniform or relatively diverse. The latter pole is sometimes referred to as 'free variation', a term which my colleagues and I tend to avoid since we doubt the validity of its implications. Finally, this type of diversity may be a property of the individual (as when Mr X vacillates between /saiˈkɔlədʒi/ and /psaiˈkɔlədʒi/ without this reflecting any such variation in society) or it may be a property of society itself (as for instance the variation between /iðə/ and /aiðə/ which need not affect a Mr Y who says only /aiðə/).

The lower limb of Fig. 2 concerns attitude—a reminder that someone's attitude to usage may have a by no means simple rela-tion to his actual usage, either natural or elicited, habitual or potential. Attitudes to usage seem to us to reflect three potentially independent but often intimately interacting factors. A person may have strong beliefs about what forms he habitually uses; and he may also have strong views on the forms that ought to be used. These may be in harmony or he may confess that he believes them to be in conflict. But we must all realize that our beliefs about our own usage by no means necessarily correspond to the actual facts of our usage—as our wives or children or other unkindly frank observers are liable to remind us from time to time. Moreover, we may tolerate usage in others that corresponds neither to what we think we say ourselves nor to what we think is most commendable.

At which point it may be expected that I should tackle the vexed question of the relation between actual usage and opinion about the most commendable usage. What can linguistics do, one may ask, to maintain or improve the quality of everyday usage? Most linguists this century have tended to use linguistic insights to show that the whole notion of maintaining or improving the quality of a language is misconceived. Very properly. Language fulfils its role to no small extent by the very fact that its users are able to change it. Linguists have therefore rightly poured scorn on those who have stood Canute-like against waves of change on principle. In December 1969 a member of the House of Lords wrote what is a typical protest to *The Times:*

> It seems that the American 'this' has become established when the word 'that' should properly be used.
>   Now one finds that in almost every other sentence . . . the word 'viable' occurs. I have always understood that the word referred to the capability of a living creature to maintain life. Is its new use another Americanism? Surely, to refer to a business, an industry, a film . . . being 'viable' is nonsense?

If we can set aside the suspicion that the main basis for irritation here is the influence of America (or perhaps a more laudable dislike of cliché and 'OK' jargon), the protest seems to stem from the fact that etymologically *viable* is related (through French *vie*) to Latin *vita.* But of course this gets us nowhere. We do not attempt to be governed by etymological meanings with words like *pen*, *pert* or *pending*, and presumably the noble critic allows himself to call a play *lively*, to say that there is no *life* in British industry, and to insist that it is *vital* to use English correctly—though no danger to life and limb is conceivable.

It is right that linguistics should not be invoked in the interests of so dubiously motivated a conservationism: right indeed that it should actually be used to give some reassurance to people who might be inhibited in the natural use of English by eminent protesters of this kind. But this does not mean that linguistics is committed on principle to any rigorous insistence on laissez-faire in matters of language use. Just as linguistic scholarship helps us to understand why change is inevitable, so the insights of linguistics can make us more alert in what we are saying or writing, so that we can avoid ambiguity or obscurity, anticipate irrelevant or unwanted overtones and *doubles entendres* (as in the questionnaire which asked 'How many people do you employ, broken down by sex?'), and achieve our objective more efficiently by well-formed and efficient phraseology, elegant and precise choice of words, sensitive and effective control of metaphor. We should not, for example, have to wrestle with clumsiness, involving trivial ambiguity, like the following sentence on 'the pill':

> All the present preparations contain a mixture of two synthetic hormones, which appear to suppress the secretion by the pituitary gland in the brain of a substance which plays a crucial part in the process of ovulation. (*Sunday Times*, 26 July 1964)

Or we may consider a more serious infelicity where—without obscurity of expression—there was genuine ambiguity. In connection with the decision whether or not to sell a house to a coloured immigrant, a builder's statement was reported as follows:

> We would not jeopardise our business by selling a house to you. (*The Times*, 18 June 1969)

Especially on so grave an issue, a user of English ought to be aware of the two structural possibilities here, the one involving conditional *would*, the other volitional:

> We would not jeopardise our business if we sold a house to you.
> We would not be willing to sell a house to you and so jeopardise our business.

Let me illustrate also the point I made about control of metaphor. A metaphor involves simultaneously a *paradigmatic* relation between the literal element it replaces and the figurative one it introduces, and a *syntagmatic* relation between the literal and metaphorical elements in the linguistic environment.[4] Thus 'the seeds of discord' must be understood as 'the initial signs, a growing murmur, the first spark of discord': but the effectiveness of this relation depends on the syntagmatic relations and we must not go on to speak of the seeds of discord rumbling in the background or bursting into flame. Obviously. But unfortunately, the mixed or wasted metaphor is not always so easy to avoid, and there is a real difficulty in that we can forget or not even know what degree of 'life' a metaphor possesses for other members of our speech community. Even Hamlet could speak of taking arms against a sea of troubles.

Last September, when it was clear that Herr Brandt was about to become Chancellor, the *Daily Express* commented on

> the tense and almost certainly squalid political horse-trading which will inflict Bonn over the next few days. (30 September 1969)

If *inflict* (which requires a human subject) is an error for *infect* or *afflict* (with their implication of disease or disaster) the syntagmatic relation with *horse-trading* is unsatisfactory—and it is little better if we are meant to understand 'which [events] will inflict [on] Bonn', or if *inflict* is an error for the semantically more vacuous *affect*.

A more interesting example of rhetorical misfire because of metaphor appeared in the opening of a leading article on the Pinkville massacre. The point at issue was whether one was being disloyal to the United States in showing horror at the alleged atrocities in Vietnam. The article began thus:

> There is a treason worse than criticism of governments. It is the treason that betrays the values for which one's country stands.
> (*Sunday Times*, 30 November 1969)

The intended metaphorical climax of the second sentence is linguistically well-formed. The *moral lapse* which departs from the traditionally upheld values is paradigmatically replaced by 'treason' which is given a congruent syntagmatic relation with 'betrays', and so the offence is made more vivid and serious. Or it should be. Unfortunately the climactic metaphor has been preceded by a sentence which, although presumably intended to affirm literal treason, unhappily undermines the succeeding metaphor by using it in a diluted and figurative sense. The first sentence thus says '*treason* is here defined as a mere anti-government criticism', and we need not be surprised that in place of a climactic metaphor in the second sentence, we get bathos and no metaphor at all.

This laborious exposition is tedious and bathetic itself, but my point has been merely to claim that a linguistic analysis of 'poor' English can point to ways in which we can use our language more effectively and more enjoyably. The message of linguistics on the native language was useful enough when it was largely confined to condemning the pedantries of prescriptive grammar. It can be made constructive in the normal educational process.

Even more obviously, it has a constructive contribution to make in therapy for the linguistically abnormal. The miracle of a Helen Keller or a Christy Brown brings home to us the potential of the deprived individual when once the mechanism of language can be brought into operation. But when we see the thousands of children who remain deprived of language powers or the adults who have been so deprived by accident or illness, we are humiliated by the realization of how little we yet understand the means by which language is learnt, the way in which semantic and syntactic rules operate in the human brain, how little we understand the very nature of language itself. In the past fifty years enormous strides have been made in the diagnosis of articulatory defects and in the construction of therapeutic drills precisely directed at the specific malarticulation detected. Where the breakthrough is needed is in the understanding of the deeper strata of linguistic organization, and here we look for fruitful co-operation between linguistics and psychological medicine.[5]

It is commonly regarded as a triumph to have the last word, but there are grave disadvantages when this means trying to find something new to add when thirteen distinguished people have already had their say. They have harvested and led away the corn, as Chaucer puts it,

> And I come after, glenynge here and there,
> And am ful glad if I may fynde an ere
> Of any goodly word that they han left.

Rather this, at any rate, than attempt a resounding peroration. All the same, we might for a moment reflect where we have arrived in our study of linguistics and where we might further direct our thoughts after these lectures.

One of the fruits of the course must surely be a wiser, sadder awareness of language's complexity and of our abiding ignorance. This is not to belittle the profound thought that generations of linguists have applied to human language, or their solid achievements, but rather to adopt a posture of proper humility in the face of all that still challenges us. If the degree of deeper understanding these lectures have conveyed leads only to a keener sensibility, a greater tolerance of language variety, and less rigid preconceptions about the uniqueness or inviolability of a national standard language, they will have served a valuable enough purpose. A realization of the almost spiritual relation between a person and the language he speaks is essential if languages and dialects are not to mutate grotesquely from badges of pride to barriers of hate and fear. The potential for harm can be seen in

Belgium's language riots and the terrible immolations in Madras: but it can be seen nearer home in the recent demonstrations for Welsh and—more insidiously—in the continued promotion of vaudeville 'comedy' where the humour lies in peculiarities of immigrants' English which can be made to seem as uproariously funny as hunchbacks, bearded ladies or the mentally ill were to our great-grandfathers.

We need only a little linguistics to give us enough ability to observe other people's language with intelligent interest rather than the scornful rejection that is born of ignorance and fear. And I do not think 'fear' is too strong a word. There is no form of xenophobia more irrational than its application to what we significantly call our *own* language, our *mother tongue*. Impassioned but impracticable plans for repatriation of linguistic immigrants have been repeatedly made since the sixteenth century, and post-imperial insecurities have not reduced such urges. A society which could accept the need by some to wear linguistic badges such as the accents associated with Oxford or Harvard is disturbed that others want to express a comparable identity through 'Soul Talk'.

Add to this not merely the emergence of American English; the reluctant admission that this implies the existence of *British* English; distant strains of 'Strine' from down under; talk in Dublin about the standards of Hiberno-English; and it is not surprising that the dissolution of empire has been accompanied by fears about the balkanization of English. Add to that again complaints that block language like 'probe', 'bid' and 'cut' is proceeding beyond the headlines to everyday speech, and we have the basis for fears that English is being reduced to a sort of pidgin. 'No word not in current kindergarten use,' writes Miss Nancy Mitford (*The Listener*, 16 May 1968), 'may be introduced into the dialogue of a film. When working on a script I once wrote "ineluctable"; I was told to take it out at once as nobody would know what it meant'.

Again, we need only a little linguistics to sharpen our observation sufficiently to know whether these fears are justified or not. Besides the fissiparous tendencies that are natural to language (they produced Spanish, French and Rumanian out of Latin, for example), English is responding to powerful counteractive tendencies of a centripetal kind that result from the special conditions of the modern world: the political affiliation of the English-speaking countries, the ease and speed of modern communications, the democratization of education, and the trend to uniformity in material culture, to mention some of the obvious factors. In many ways, we are linguistically much less insular in Britain than we

were even as little as twenty years ago, having learnt to respond
with great immediacy not merely to American English but to the
English of Australia, the West Indies, Africa and the Indian subcontinent—not to speak of the English of Merseyside. Inevitably,
this has meant our adopting many words from these varieties of
English—especially American English of course—but the spread
of language habits has not been a one-way process. Through
broadcasting, books and the British news-agencies, we have continued to increase the world's familiarity with British English;
and even the all-powerful American English has yielded to our
influence in certain fields—not least, the language of pop. In short,
although a century ago it seemed that English might indeed break
up into different languages as the Romance group did, more recent
tendencies have been in the reverse direction. A word no sooner
becomes fashionable in San Francisco than it is equally so in
Bradford and Brisbane. Rather than talk of English being balkan-
ized or pidginized, it might be more accurate to think of its being
homogenized. And if this particular image helps us to realize that
British English is no longer the cream of English, that we have
instead the concept of a language measured out in labelled cartons
all of which are guaranteed equally creamy, we may end these
lectures with an analogy which has implications for our sociolinguistic health. At any rate, we may hope that there is no
analogue to Strontium 90.

NOTES

1. S. Greenbaum, *Verb-Intensifier Collocations in English* (The
   Hague 1970), esp. pp. 73 ff.
2. R. M. Kempson, & R. Quirk, 'Controlled Activation of Latent
   Contrast', *Language* 47 (1971).
3. S. Greenbaum, & R. Quirk, *Elicitation Experiments in English:
   Studies in Use and Attitude* (London 1970), pp. 1 ff.
4. G. N. Leech, *A Linguistic Guide to English Poetry* (London 1969),
   pp. 150 ff.
5. Cf. Report of the Committee of Enquiry into the Speech Therapy
   Services (HMSO: London 1972), esp. Ch. 10.

12 On Knowing English

There are two ways of 'knowing' any piece of language. One is the linguist's knowledge of how the piece of language is constructed: that is, what elements are involved and what goes on when they are brought together. The other is the language user's knowledge of how to construct the piece of language when he needs to use it or how it is to be understood when he hears someone else use it. These two kinds of knowing, it need hardly be mentioned, by no means necessarily go together. There are many foreign linguists who can scarcely be excelled at learned discourse about English grammar but whose knowledge of English (in my second sense) is less good than that of an average London child of nine. At the same time, many of those whose knowledge of English is most impressive—poets, novelists, orators—are unable to explain the structure of the simplest sentence: some even boast about it. Sir Winston Churchill was perhaps exceptional in believing that his ability to use English was related to his theoretical knowledge of the language. In a recent issue of the *Michigan Quarterly Review*, he is reported to have given this piece of advice in Ann Arbor may years ago: 'Verify your quotations and avoid split infinitives'.

The confounding of these two kinds of knowing has, of course, bedevilled our teaching of English for generations, and the most impassioned cries that children know little English are reduced to impotence through conflicting interpretations (cf. pp. 84 ff. above). This is true even of Alexander Barclay's tirade on the subject 450 years ago in a section of his long adaptation of Brandt's *Narrenschiff* entitled 'Of vnprofytable stody':

> But moste I marveyll of other folys blynde
> Whiche in dyvers scyencis ar fast laborynge
> Both daye and nyght with all theyr herte and mynde
> But of gramer knowe they lytyll or no thynge

An earlier version of this paper was read to the Royal Society of Arts on 18th May 1966.

Whiche is the grounde of all lyberall cunnynge
Yet many ar besy in Logyke and in lawe
Whan all theyr gramer is skarsly worth a strawe.[1]

Whatever Barclay meant by knowing 'gramer', our work on the
Survey of English Usage at University College London concerns
the second kind: it is a study of the native user's proficiency, and
we only hope Barclay would not think of it as an 'vnprofytable
stody'. Certainly, less ink has been spilt on this than on the first
kind of knowing—no doubt because a person's ability to speak
his own language is so easily taken for granted. The first lisped
words of the infant seem miraculous to a parent, and rightly so,
but paradoxically the nearer he comes to a full knowledge of the
language the less miraculous it sounds. To say 'Bikky for baby' at
two earns the highest rewards; to say at seven, 'If I can have
another marron glacé, I'll go straight to bed' earns only a black
look. The language ability is taken for granted: only the acquired
sense of blackmail is noticed.

Yet am I not exaggerating? How much is taken for granted?
There is another paradox here, for beside the unmarvelled accep-
tance of the native speaker's proficiency, there is a long tradition
of inquiry into the facts of usage and a long-standing demand for
the results as incapsulated in such volumes as Fowler's *Modern
English Usage*, recently revised by the late Sir Ernest Gowers.[2]
Why, or in what respect, should Fowler and Gowers have to tell
us how to use a language we already 'know'? In attempting to
answer this question, I should like to begin by looking at some of
the ways in which language structure can go wrong.

(1) The is empty box little.

There is nothing in Fowler about sentences like this, and quite
rightly; whatever 'knowing English' means, it certainly means
that we have no difficulty in knowing how to avoid such scrambled
nonsense.

(2) Cricket paints boys.

This is more like English (superficially it is rather like the fully
acceptable *Beauty delights men*), but we do not say such things
and avoiding them needs no teaching. If, however, it is felt that
these examples are unenlightening because they are so obviously
contrived and so unlikely to occur, let us look at a comparable
example which appeared in an intelligent newspaper article:

(3) This work is taking two main directions. The first consists of
further investigations of existing suggestions, such as statistical service

into causative factors other than smoking, and further tests on labora-
tory, namely what group production of combustion of tobacco. The
second is more factual work on a chemical products of tobacco of
combustion.   (Qt 57.28/6)

Confronted with such material, we are not inclined to criticize the
writer's English, nor are we likely to think that here are new con-
structions that we have not encountered before (though we are in
the habit of taking precisely this humble attitude when we meet
strange *words*, as opposed to strange *arrangements* of words).
Instead, we are convinced that here is some kind of accident—a
mechanical accident, having nothing to do with language.

   In the next example, the situation is only slightly different:

   (4) I am come here since five years.

Here again we do not expect to find in Fowler the rules explaining
what is wrong and how to avoid grammar of this kind. Although
we have all heard and politely responded to sentences like this, the
speaker has always been a foreigner, and whatever rules are necessary to correct him on such points, we do not know them ourselves: we only know they are not needed by any native speaker.

   (5a) Him and her was there alone.
    b) He don't need no help.

Now at last we have sentences that native speakers are capable of
uttering and most of us could make a fair attempt at stating the
rules that are being broken. Yet here again Fowler has very little
to say, for the sound practical reason that anyone literate enough
to consult a book on usage is already in command of standard
English, to which these expressions are almost as foreign as (4) is.

   Up to this point, then, 'knowing' our language means that we
are in little danger of producing any of the exemplified deviations.
It is beyond this point that less can be taken for granted.

   (6a) He's different than me.
    b) Between you and I, she's silly.
    c) Who did you give it to?

Here are usages commonly heard in the speech of the educated,
and while we may stoutly defend our right to any or all of them,
we must acknowledge that they will be just as stoutly condemned
by our neighbours. But whether we use or avoid them, we know
the rules that are being broken and we would be confident that
they are described rather fully in Fowler. It is interesting to speculate on why clear and known rules should in these instances be
freely broken while the unconscious and obscure rules relating to

(1) or (4) should not be broken, but there are even thornier problems ahead:

> (7a) For everyone to have walked out would not have surprised me.
> b) More candidates applied than we have places to offer them.
> c) These people have a tendency for their hair to fall out.

The difference between (6) and (7) is not merely that the latter can
appear in print while the former tend to vanish blessedly into the
unseen silence beyond the sound waves. A more important difference is that if we suspect that something is wrong in (7) we can
find little comfort in appeal to codified rule. Moreover, it is
difficult to find a simple rectification: if we are dissatisfied, we have
to recast the sentences rather radically. Yet each is perfectly comprehensible, suggesting that they have in some sense an adequate
structure.

Finally, consider the following:

> (8) The man who came to the door when the policeman who lives
> nearby in a tumbledown house called with his faithful dog which is
> lame because of a car accident on account of which the driver was
> prosecuted for having a vehicle which had no roadworthiness certi-
> ficate although he was acquitted was drunk.

In this breathless example, we have the paradox of a sentence
being quite definitely unacceptable although it does not embody a
single feature which is in any way grammatically dubious: a sentence which seems to be confused and obscure but which examination shows to be perfectly coherent and even simple: a sentence
which would be as troublesome to the speaker trying to frame it as
to the listener trying to grasp it (cf. Ch. 10).

In (6), (7), and (8), then, we see areas of usage in which a native
speaker's proficiency cannot be taken for granted. It is in such
areas that the native speaker has traditionally sought help from
the handbooks. Let us now look more closely at the nature of the
problems involved.

We have noted that some sentences appear to be so easy, *The
little box is empty*, that getting them wrong is almost incon-
ceivable. On the other hand, (8) shows that a sentence made up of
parts which are almost as simple can rapidly become difficult to
grasp as more parts are added. Linguists in recent years have seen
this problem in terms of the metaphor 'depth',[3] and it has been
suggested that we analyse sentences as branching tree structures,
thus:

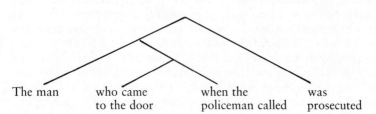

and that we can then estimate the probable limit of tolerable complexity in relation to the number of *nodes* or branching-points in the tree. Although a great deal depends on the type of branching involved, we can be reasonably sure that in general our control over both forming and understanding a sentence increases sharply with the number of nodes and that our teaching tradition in its informal disapproval of over-complexity is soundly based. It is by no means unusual for a speaker to get 'lost' if he embarks on a sentence with a fairly ambitious structure:

(9) /I'm sûre # that when /this was wrìtten # . al/though it's :written # – in a /sénse # . des/cribing the de:velopment of a mán # you know *m* they /went with :songs to the :battle they were :young *m* # and :sò ·on # – is des/cribing the de:velopment of a mān # and /his sudden dèath # – the /real effèct # . /is not the :literal effèct # the /rèal ef·fect # is the /meta!phòrical ·one # . ((it)) is the /mèmory # which *m* /shall not grow òld # *m* #[4]

(5b.2–22)

Since my point is that any educated person is liable to produce this and the other examples from Survey texts that I shall quote, it would be an invidious irrelevance to identify sources on the present occasion. Full information on the linguistic material and on our informants (who must all have had a university education) is of course preserved in the Survey files at University College.

One's ability to revise and expunge in writing means that examples as gross as (9) are rarely found in print. They may be found, however, in unrevised manuscript material where (perhaps by reason of the delay between composition and expression, thinking and writing) it takes only a small degree of complexity to make us lose our way. The following is a sentence opening a correspondence between an English lecturer and someone he had never met:

(10) I am trying to determine how far the new thinking about English language teaching represented by your book *The Use of English* and your draft A-level syllabus. It seemed to me that you . . .(QL6.66.11/4)

In one structural respect, indeed, the result of getting lost through grammatical complexity is commonly seen even in print: I refer to the weakening of grammatical government, when the governing and governed items are separated. There are examples of this in (6): *Who did you give it to?* (where *To who did you give it?* is unlikely to occur) and *Between you and I* (where *Between I and you* is unthinkable), though there are other factors to be considered in this instance.[5] While it is unlikely that an M.P. would say 'The increase are attributed', *Hansard* last year reported one as asking

> (11) . . . the Minister of Health if he will state the number of deaths which have been caused by leukaemia in each of the last five years; and to what causes the increase in the incidence of this disease since the end of the Second World War are attributed.[6]

I should like to concentrate, however, on one consequence of complexity that appears to give even the most fluent native users of English special difficulty. This is the process of abbreviation that takes place when simple structures are conjoined to make complex ones, a process which necessarily makes complex structures less 'explicit' though curiously (as we shall see in a moment) not less easily understandable. Instead of saying *Mary washed the clothes and Mary ironed the clothes*, we say *Mary washed and ironed the clothes*, which requires the listener to assume that *Mary* is the subject of *ironed* and *the clothes* the object of *washed*. He is expected to understand the whole sentence in this way and to dismiss, for instance, the possibility that it could mean 'Mary washed [i.e., herself] and then she ironed the clothes'. Similarly, instead of *John tried so that John would finish the job but John did not finish the job*, the rules of English partly oblige and partly permit the several abbreviations that result in *John tried to finish the job but he didn't*. Here *John* is assumed to be the subject of *finish*, *he* to be a substitute for *John* and *didn't* a substitute for *didn't finish the job* (not for *didn't try*). The sentence *John tried but he didn't* would carry quite different assumptions about both *he* and *didn't*, but again they are assumptions that are provided for in our 'knowledge' of English.

It is noteworthy that, in varieties of English (notably, the language of statutes) where maximum explicitness is aimed at, ordinary readers find such language harder to understand than the highly elliptical and assumptive language that might *a priori* seem more obscure. While other factors (notably, tree-structure complexity of the kind already discussed) contribute to the difficulty of the following passage, the difficulty partly lies in the full explicitness:

(12) For the purposes of this Part of this Schedule a person over pensionable age, not being an insured person, shall be treated as an employed person if he would be an insured person were he under pensionable age and would be an employed person were he an insured person.

(National Insurance Act, 1964, 1st Schedule, Part II)

Reduced explicitness (or increased abbreviation) is perhaps most commonly introduced by co-ordination, and it is not therefore surprising that sentences involving co-ordination provide common difficulties:

(13a) discrimination between the tax on distributed and undistributed profits.   (8fa.1–28)
   b) there remains a discrepancy between the latest value of /n'/ in comparison with that of /n"/   (8a.2.166–2)
   c) . . . he is capable and willing to pay for the privilege.
                                                        (Qt 63. 29/10)
   d) the views I've expréssed # in /Párliament # in the /cóuntry # on /bróadcasting # and on /télevision #   (5b.51–6)
   e) Mr. —— said Canada and Australia would also lose under agreements which no one knew would be met or what they contained.   (Qt 62.22/9)
   f) Barrow boys calling their wares and that they are the best but cheap.[7]

The last of these is not from a Survey text but from a G.C.E. script, and it is worth noting that a feature penalized in school examinations remains a source of difficulty throughout our lives.

A special case of trouble with co-ordination appears when comparative structures are also involved:

(14a) an :equally serious or :even m # "!mòre serious crime situátion # than /we do in this !!còuntry #   (5b.51–47)
   b) in :some cases . !wòrse # and in /some cases not so bădly # as /wè do #   (5b.51–45)
   c) the /more . you . de!vèlop # [. . .] . the /more your a:bĭlity #
                                                        (5b.2–33)

In two of these examples, *than* and *as* respectively appear to be used as though either was the appropriate linkage with both positive and comparative terms in the degree system. Now, of course, there are languages in which a single particle does so serve (German *als*, French *que*, for example). Since English examples like (14) are so common and since they are so immediately comprehensible (and not at first sight reprehensible), it might be suggested that in some sense an underlying structure exists in English too where no distinction is made. Here is another sense in which the metaphor of *depth* is used by linguists.[8] We may postulate that in our internal mechanism for constructing sentences, we work with highly abstract entities which we may think of as elements of 'deep structure' and that most of the social conventions of wording and arrangement that we usually call 'grammar' concern rather the 'surface structure' in which the abstract entities are actually realized in speech and writing. In the present instance, we may suppose that the particle linking a term in the degree system with its related clause is a single feature in deep structure, only differentiated as *than* or *as* in surface structure.

There is similar evidence to support the hypothesis of abstract 'sandhi exponents', as they have been called,[9] in the following material:

(15a) /courts shòuld be empówered # *m* /subject to :certain
    reser:vations and qualificátions # *m* # . in im/pō[/sīng #] # .
    /sentences . . .   (5b.51–3)

  b) my /own . ə:m – – ə: !prèference # – *p* I /think *p* # would be
     fōr – ex!ploring . . .   (S.1c.11–46)

  c) ((there's *p* # *f q* /no)) !pōint # *f* # *q* # /you sēe # of of
     /asking *a* for . . .   (S.1c.11–14)

  d) remembering ə . :đi: particular ″dáy # for which this /prog-
     ramme is to be héld #   (5b.2–12)

  e) had to be restricted to groups of lines rather than for individual
     reflections.   (8a.2.166–2)

Let us assume, for instance, that in deep grammar the relation between whatever corresponds to *This has no point* and whatever corresponds to *Someone asks something* is represented by a non-finitization process together with an undifferentiated particle abstraction, only differentiated in surface structure, as in *What is the point of asking?* beside *There's no point in asking.* This would help to explain both the mis-selection in (15c) and the relative irrelevance of the mis-selection. The hypothesis has a still clearer application to (15b), since *preference* can collocate with *for* plus noun or (in certain circumstances) with *to* plus verb; the underlying neutralization of the distinction in this particular instance (*preference for an exploration* and *preference to explore*) is easily appreciated. The other instances should perhaps be studied in relation to a wider 'deep semantics' to which we shall presently allude, though it may be noted in passing that in (15e) we are once more concerned with a type of comparative structure.

Let us therefore pursue the matter with reference to further material involving comparatives:

(16a) I /don't *m* # ″fìnd my·self # *m* /getting. /getting as as as
    m′ !ìrritated # *m*′ # *a* I'm /more ⁻amùsed you knów #
                (S.1c.11–52)

b) [the amity] is . perhaps !hardly ex:ēeeded # ɔ: than /by . the
   [loyalty]   (5b.16–30)
c) my :ordinary :decent :brĕast # is a /little :different than
   Ròbert's #   (5b.1–5)

I have discussed elsewhere[10] the relation of *different* to the comparison system, and for the present we may look only at the
second example. We might explain this rather muddled expression by saying that in the deep structure there were entities corresponding to something like *Loyalty is great* and *Amity is greater
but not much greater*, thus *Amity is not much greater than loyalty*.
Part of the surface structure corresponding to this appears in the
selection of *than*, but for the most part the whole of the abstract
deep structure has been given an entirely different surface realization involving the verb *exceed*. This example, in fact, interestingly
suggests how the deep structure is compounded of grammatical
and semantic abstractions, with perhaps little to correspond to the
rather sharp distinction that exists between vocabulary and
grammar in surface structure. Such a semantic deep structure
would account also for the following:

(17) Mr. —— said that although there might be evidence of premarital
     intercourse by young people there was little to suggest that this
     pattern persisted after marriage.   (Qt 65. 26/2)

where this can be read (and probably was read by thousands) with
a full understanding of the individual words and yet with a full
understanding also of the whole sentence presumably intended by
the speaker. From this point of view, it may even seem pedantic to
have the absurdity pointed out. In other words, the absurdity is
perhaps in an important sense superficial: the speaker intended
(and most readers doubtless understood) a deep semantic unit
'illicit intercourse' which is applicable to both unmarried and
married, and it is only the surface realization of this entity that
accidentally restricts it.

I should like to take the deep structure hypothesis a little further.
We all learn quite early to abbreviate two sentences into one of
the form *Shaving this morning, I had an idea*, which depends on
a firm convention between speaker and hearer that the implicit
subject of *shaving* is the same as the explicit subject of *had*. Thus
the sentence *Shaving this morning, the car broke down* would be
nonsense. Actually instances of the so-called 'dangling participle'
are not usually nonsense, however:

(18a) Crossing the stile, which usually makes its appearance at the end
      of a lane, some cows come into view.

    b) Moving over the next field, and climbing a small hill, a farm yard appears nestling in a small copse.
    c) Besides going to watch football, there are usually tennis-courts.
    d) As well as having flower-beds, there are hot-houses, too.[11]

and they are by no means always pounced on, as these were, as signs of bad English. At a recent meeting of this Society, an example appeared in an admirably clear Basic English booklet that was distributed; it read: 'Coming to the special need of science for an international language, in no field is this need clearer, most important, or more frequently voiced.'[12]

What is it, we may ask, that makes the actual instances in (18) less absurd than my example, *Shaving this morning, the car broke down*? It will be noticed that if the last had read either *As well as there being flower-beds, there are hot-houses* or *As well as having flower-beds, one has hot-houses*, the writer would have escaped criticism. In other words, the verbs have no literal precision; they are surface devices to express a very general idea of 'existence'. As such, they are synonymous and their selection may even have been deliberate in a mistaken attempt to introduce a kind of elegant variation such as one is encouraged to cultivate in the matter of vocabulary selection. All the verbs in (18) are in fact to some extent existential,[13] and we should notice that the first would be importantly less acceptable if the second part read 'some cows come slowly to be milked', and on the other hand subtly more acceptable if it read 'some cows come into *my* view', thus explicitly introducing the required subject of *crossing*.

But probably nowhere does the conflict between deep and surface structure give more trouble than in the matter of number,[14] where the rather sharp line dividing singular and plural for all but a few nouns like *committee* (and those chiefly in British English) is palpably unsatisfactory for handling the much subtler number distinctions that apparently exist in deep structure. Let us first look at some examples involving the old problem of 'All the children put their hands up' where the sentence does not make it clear (and cannot easily be emended so as to make clear) whether each child put up one of his hands, as though to attract attention, or both of his hands, as though to obey an armed robber. Beside the surface neutralization of the distinction between 'One boy put up his hand' and 'One boy put up his hands' when the subject is made plural ('Two boys put up their hands'), there is evidence that the distinction is preserved in deep structure, rather as though one were to say 'Two boys put up their hand':

(19a) that *l* /raises these savage feelings in our ordinary . :decent
      brèasts # *l* #   (5b.1.5)

b) this par/ticular :group of cóuncillors # . /in Cróydon #
en/tirely on their own bát #   (5b.1.20)
c) /young sòldiers # . /killed in bàttle # . ((that)) /spent nearly !all
their life in prepa:ràtion #   (5b.2.23)

We noted above (p. 129) that co-ordination was a source of
trouble to the native user of English. Not surprisingly, one aspect
of such trouble is the number system:

(20a) . . . and now she, and everyone present, was ready to break it.
                                                               (6.2.98–1)
b) With Mr Eborebelosa it's his colour, and with this other one it's
his class, that come into the picture.   (6.2.92–1)

The sentences *She was ready* and *Everyone present was ready* can
be co-ordinated in two ways. In one way, there would be no
hesitation in selecting a plural verb: *She and everyone present
were ready.* The other way involves a subtler co-ordination in
which one of the co-ordinate units is subordinated to the other;
the commas in (20a) are an attempt to represent this subordina-
tion which in speech would probably be realized in reduced
prominence, but of course a less objectionable way of expressing
the contrast would have been to select *like* or *as well as* which,
unlike *and*, exercise no verbal concord requirement. As for (20b),
it seems reasonable to hypothesize that no number conflict need
arise in a deep structure where plurality is dominant: two things,
as it were, come into the picture—one person's colour and the
other person's class. Unfortunately, selection of the cleft sentence
structure in realizing the co-ordination has forced on the writer a
difficult choice between *come* and *comes*. It is worth noting,
incidentally, that here, as with several of the other examples being
considered, a possible factor inhibiting establishment of a solution to such problems is the relative rarity of their relevance in
realization. That is to say, it will always matter—as with (20a)—
whether an item in co-ordination is subordinated or not, but only
with a small minority of verb forms does the distinction affect
concord: compare *She and everyone present wanted to break it*
and *She, and everyone present, wanted to break it*.

We need scarcely pause over the next examples:

(21a) just to show he understood the finer points of those sort of
things.   (6.4.54–3)
b) "/nòne of my cólleagues # have /said !ănything # . . .
                                                               (5b.1.50)

One should just note that, despite singular features on the surface,
both of these are well-established in retaining their deeper plurality
in surface grammar too. One might also note that, even without

the plural post-modifier in (21b), *none* would quite usually take a plural verb: *None have come*. In this respect the grammar of *none* is interestingly different from that of *nobody* and *everybody*:

> (22a) Nobody ever behaves quite the same in private as they do in public . . .   (6.3.201–1)
>   b) /everybody :in a housing estáte # is /made alike by :one fàctor # and /like it or not it :is a :fàct # – /that they are líving # u/pon the chárity # . . .   (5b.1.17)

But although *nobody* and *everybody* take a singular verb, it is probably their 'deeper' plurality that determines the use of the reference pronoun *they* in each example. One says 'probably' here because an alternative deep motivation might be the sex-independence of the corresponding abstract entities which cannot be matched in the English singular pronoun system.

The question of number with nouns like *committee* involves some fairly clearly established conventions. When used as singulars, they have singular verbs and are referred to by the non-personal pronoun *it* and the non-personal relative pronoun *which*; when used as plurals, we use a plural verb, *they* and *who*. The frequency of vacillation in actual use, however, can be seen in:

> (23a) /Germany is ″!nòt an independent nátion # it is ″/still contròlled #   (5b.1.54)
>   b) !problem of running :Gèrmany # /let them run themsélves #
>   (5b.1.53)
>   c) /Croydon ″isn't sàying # . /if you're earning :twenty pounds a wèek # you must /pay the :economic rènt # . /what they're saying ís # . . .   (5b.1.26)

It is not just attributable to the gross carelessness so often alleged but rather suggests that the distinction is not represented so cleanly in deep structure. The first two of these examples occurred within seconds of each other in a radio discussion programme, and the third suggests that neither the singular nor the plural satisfactorily represents the aggregation intended in the use of such collective nouns.

A similar but still more striking instance of conflict between deep and surface structure is to be seen in the use of countable nouns as contextually generic:

> (24a) When kept as a pet, jackdaws often takes rings and silver coins and hoard them in some secret corner.
>   b) If a child does not receive all these things disease will set in and their bodies will not develop.[15]

In these examples, the noun phrases *a pet* and *a child* are no more referentially singular than *jackdaws* and *their bodies* are referentially plural. What appear to correspond abstractly to them are entities independent of number which might correspond to their countable representatives somewhat in the way that *humanity* corresponds to *a grey-haired man*. Nor should we think that trouble with this generic usage is confined to G.C.E. candidates:

(25a) /I think the gene:ălogist # . by /telling us something about the :dĕtail # . of /some of the . !families that've . :brèd # in this /rather ?res:tricted wáy # . are /gòing to be ·able . . . (5b.2.49)

   b) because the /things which ″!shòuld interest a man móst # . are in /fact đi . :[bihi] .!is in fact đi be:haviour of other :mèn #
   (5b.2.11)

   c) the /human béing # can /do a :little !mòre # with his /intu!ìtion # . when there's ″/so many variables . . . (5b.2.7)

   d) /and that :economic rént # . /is being paid :by the com-múnity # . /by the other rátepayers # by the /taxpàyer #
   (5b.1.17)

In (25a), the immediate cause of the false concord, *the genealogist are*, has been the weakening of grammatical government by separation (as illustrated above, p. 128). But there is probably a deeper cause and we may agree that the speaker, a university professor, might equally have selected a generic formal plural, *genealogists*, in this sentence, and that in fact the semantic abstraction underlying his selection is neither singular nor plural but of an intermediate number. There is, however, nothing to correspond to this in surface structure, which enforces a quite unsatisfactory binary decision. What we have been saying is neatly illustrated in (25d) where in quick succession the speaker uses a collective, *the community*, a plural, *the other ratepayers*, and a generic singular, *the taxpayer*.

My aims in this paper have been appropriately modest in the face of the awesome and humiliating complexity of English usage. I have sought primarily, indeed, to emphasize how much is involved in 'knowing' a language, in the sense of being proficient in the use of a language. We have seen something of the bounds that can be set between those areas in which a native speaker has unerring certainty and those in which he ranges from vacillation to the dread point at which he finds himself unable to say what he needs to say, understand what he needs to understand. And finally we have devoted some time to a glimpse of some of the specific trouble spots to which my colleagues and I on the Survey of English Usage have recently been giving our attention.

NOTES

1. T. H. Jamieson, *The Ship of Fools translated by Alexander Barclay* (Edinburgh, 1874), Vol. I, p. 144.
2. See Chapter 9. On experimental inquiry into usage, see R. Quirk and J. Svartvik, *Investigating Linguistic Acceptability* (Mouton, The Hague, 1966); R. Quirk, *Essays on the English Language* (London, 1968), Ch. 17.
3. Cf. V. Yngve, 'The Depth Hypothesis', *Proceedings of Symposia in Applied Mathematics*, Vol. 12 (1961), pp. 130–8; R. D. Huddleston, 'Rank and Depth', *Language* 41 (1965), esp. pp. 585f.
4. The symbol # marks the end of each intonation unit, while accents indicate the contour pattern: thus an acute accent denotes a rising tone. On these and other symbols, see further, D. Crystal and R. Quirk, *Systems of Prosodic and Paralinguistic Features* (The Hague, 1964.)
5. For example, hypercorrectness in avoiding *you and me* in verbless clauses ('Who can go? You and me?'). Note also that *He's wrong, between you and I* is somewhat more acceptable than *Put the vase between you and I*, a difference which is referable to semantics and 'depth' in the other sense discussed below.
6. *Parliamentary Debates* (HMSO, 1965), Vol. 716, No. 156, column 1089.
7. University of Cambridge, Local Examinations Syndicate: Report on the Work in English Language (Cambridge, 1957), p. 7.
8. Cf. C. F. Hockett, *A Course in Modern Linguistics* (New York, 1958), pp. 246ff; N. Chomsky, *Aspects of the Theory of Syntax* (Cambridge, Mass., 1965), esp. pp. 64 ff.
9 Y. Olsson, *On the Syntax of the English Verb* (Gothenburg, 1961), esp. pp. 55 ff.
10. *Language*, Vol. 41 (1965), p. 215.
11. University of Cambridge, ibid., p. 7.
12. E. C. Graham, *Basic English as an International Language* (London, 1962), pp. 5–6.
13. Lacking 'communicative dynamism', in J. Firbas's terms; see his 'Thoughts on the Communicative Function of the Verb', *Brno Studies in English*, Vol. I (1959), pp. 39 ff., 'On Defining the Theme in Functional Sentence Analysis', *Travaux Linguistiques de Prague*, Vol. I (1964), pp. 267 ff.
14. Cf. Barbara M. H. Strang, 'Some Aspects of S-V Concord in Present Day English', *Acta* of the Venice Conference, 1965, of the International Association of University Professors of English.
15. University of Cambridge, ibid., p. 8.